4/Dec '08

Where Stories Meet

An Oral History of De-ba-jeh-mu-jig Theatre

Where Stories Meet

An Oral History of De-ba-jeh-mu-jig Theatre

Shannon Hengen

Playwrights Canada Press
Toronto • Canada

Playwrights Canada Press
The Canadian Drama Publisher
215 Spadina Avenue, Suite 230, Toronto, Ontario CANADA M5T 2C7
416-703-0013 fax 416-408-3402
orders@playwrightscanada.com • www.playwrightscanada.com

Financial support provided by the taxpayers of Canada and Ontario through the Canada
Council for the Arts and the Department of Canadian Heritage through the Book Publishing
Industry Development Programme, and the Ontario Arts Council.

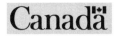 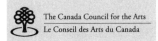

Front cover photo, "Storytelling in the Great Tipi," by Ron Berti
Production Editor/Cover design: JLArt

Library and Archives Canada Cataloguing in Publication

Hengen, Shannon Eileen
    Where stories meet : an oral history of De-ba-jeh-mu-jig Theatre / Shannon
Hengen.

Includes index.
ISBN 978-0-88754-886-4

    1. De-ba-jeh-mu-jig Theatre Group--History. 2. De-ba-jeh-mu-jig Theatre
Group. 3. De-ba-jeh-mu-jig Theatre Group--Biography. 4. Native theater--
Ontario--Wikwemikong Unceded Indian Reserve--History. I. Title.

PN2305.O6H45 2007   792.089'970713135   C2007-902106-9

First edition: May 2007.
Printed and bound by Canadian Printco at Scarborough, Canada.

The publisher and the interviewer would like to acknowledge those who agreed to have their interviews published in this book.

for Karl Skierszkan

and

in memory of Herman A. Hengen
(1907–1975)

with special thanks to Audrey Wemigwans

*The artist is the creation,
and the performance is the celebration.*

*—From The Four Directions Creation Process,
De-ba-jeh-mu-jig Theatre Group*

Contents

Where Stories Meet

An Oral History of De-ba-jeh-mu-jig Theatre

Through speaking, hearing, and retelling [stories], we affirm our relationship with our nations, our tribal communities, our family networks. We begin to understand our position in the long history of our people. Indeed, we become the stories we tell, don't we? We become the people and places of our past because our identity is created, our perspective formed, of their telling....

We learn our role in story and are meant to carry that role into daily life. We have a response-ability and a responsibility to the telling. We can and we must make the story together.

—Kimberley M. Blaeser, "Writing voices speaking: Native authors and an oral aesthetic," 54, 64

Some dark thing tells me that I will never feel at home on this land until I know how my own stories intertwine with the stories of those who were inhabiting the land when my ancestors arrived.

Frances Greenslade, *A Pilgrim in Ireland*, 126–27

— • – • —

De-ba-jeh-mu-jig Theatre of Wikwemikong Unceded Indian Reserve is a place where stories meet. Its very name is a Cree and Ojibway mix meaning story tellers, and during its twenty-three years the theatre has brought together many tellers of tales. Those who made and are making the theatre tell their stories in this book. Although those quoted here are typically modest about their accomplishments, this book will try to show that their work in recreating a traditional past enables a future so promising that it can only be guessed at. By telling Aboriginal stories, De-ba-jeh-mu-jig brings together old and new, traditional and mainstream, Native and non-Native. To quote the mandate from the theatre's website: "De-ba-jeh-mu-jig Theatre Group is a professional community-based non-profit organization, dedicated to the vitalization of the Anishinaabeg culture, language, and heritage, through education and the sharing of original creative expression with both Native and non-Native people."

Situated on Manitoulin Island, Ontario, the theatre attracts audiences of summer tourists for its annual mainstage performance but it also tours extensively to reserves, schools, and other theatre spaces in Canada and the U.S. In recent years it has developed an innovative training program for young potential theatre practitioners in areas north of Manitoulin Island, territory where the life of the theatre has lain dormant for centuries. Started as a theatre for and about youth, De-ba-jeh-mu-jig has never failed to nurture the creative life of the young Native population while drawing on the talents, reputations, and generosity of established Native theatre artists. However, as its production history will show, the theatre's work has reached out to audiences of all ages. Traditional story-telling itself does not in fact distinguish between children's and adult's stories, for the tales that we learn, tell, and retell stay with us throughout our lives, shaping us and our culture. The Artistic Directors of the theatre starting with its founder, Shirley Cheechoo, continuing through Tomson Highway, Alanis King, and Audrey Wemigwans, then current Artistic Director Joe Osawabine, current Artistic Producer Ron Berti, Board Members Marjorie and Rose Marie Trudeau are interviewed. The late Artistic Director Larry Lewis will be remembered in a brief biography.

Shirley Cheechoo

Recounting their experiences, they [traditional storytellers] illustrated how narratives that have been passed on orally for generations continue to provide a foundation for evaluating contemporary choices and for clarifying decisions made as young women, as mature adults, and during later life. Such narratives depict humans, animals, and other nonhuman beings engaged in an astonishing variety of activities and committed to mutually sustaining relationships that ensure the continuing well-being of the world. One of the many things these women taught me is that their narratives do far more than entertain. If one has optimistic stories about the past, they showed, one can draw on internal resources to survive and make sense of arbitrary forces that might otherwise seem overwhelming.

—Julie Cruikshank, *The Social Life of Stories*, xii

— • – • —

This interview took place 2 August 2000 at Shirley Cheechoo's home in M'Chigeeng (formerly West Bay), Manitoulin Island, Ontario. Thanks to the theatre's founder for so graciously providing the interview and the home.

— • – • —

SC   When I first started the theatre company, I was working with the youth in the community. It was actually called West Bay Children's Theatre. It was the year of the Festival of Sharing [1981]. The organizers of the festival asked me if I would host the theatre part of the festival and because the play we wrote for that festival was called *Respect the Voice of the Child* [by Shirley Cheechoo and Billy Merasty], we had some adults in the roles, and so we realized that the children's theatre wasn't going to work anymore. And as I was applying for funding for this play I discovered that I needed a board of directors and needed to incorporate as a non-profit organization in order to be qualified for other funding. I decided we needed to expand the theatre and include adults. Then I changed the name to De-ba-jeh-mu-jig which means "story tellers." I'd taken the Ojibway and

Cree ways of saying it which came to be De-ba-jeh-mu-jig. When I was doing the children's theatre, Blake [Debassige, Cheechoo's husband] had gotten involved so we decided that he would be on the board of directors. We just had to find other board members. But, I don't remember who they were! [Laughter.] But their names must be somewhere! I was the artistic director and I don't know how long I was the artistic director either!

SH   And then there was Tomson Highway and then Larry Lewis.

SC   Well, because I was a board member and a very active board member and president of the company, I oversaw a lot of stuff almost like the general manager of the company even though I had different artistic directors. I had different artistic directors because I always believed that when you are working in the creative process you always have to have input from other sources. But I always felt that with new blood bringing new stuff, that was more exciting than trying to hold on to the artistic director position in the company I created. My goal was to develop talent in every area of the theatre and also to concentrate on the youth.

SH   When did the children's theatre start?

SC   The West Bay Children's Theatre started in 1981.

SH   You said that the idea behind *Shadow People* [by Shirley Cheechoo] was to get people to do something about the high rate of suicide among Native boys and young men. And, what an amazing group of consultants you put together for that show.

SC   It was workshopped. Larry Lewis and several of the actors came in and workshopped the script that I had written, and we came up with *Shadow People*. Larry Lewis wasn't available to direct the play, so it was directed by Vinetta Strombergs.

SH   And you decided to do touring of these plays?

SC   Anything that has to do with the youth, it's very wise to tour because most of the issues and situations that happen on one reserve are happening on every reserve. I thought it would be best to share what we'd come up with at Debaj with other communities.

SH   You did fundraising and started applying for grants, and so you basically got all the money together for these productions?

SC   Yeah, at first. It was a lot of work.

SH And that year was 1985 and you started the theatre training workshops which were in music, mask, movement, mime, and dance. After each of these workshops, was there a little performance?

SC Usually every time we did some kind of workshop or even if it was in writing we would do a reading just to show the community what we were doing. We always wanted to show the community exactly what the theatre was developing at the time so that when we asked for their support, they knew what they were supporting.

SH Young people were interested in the workshops? Was it just young people?

SC No, once the theatre became De-ba-jeh-mu-jig, adults and young people were included in the whole system. The real goal was to develop new talent, and not just actors but in all areas of the theatre. The main goal was to develop new artistic directors, just like I said before so that there is always new blood going into the theatre and in the creative process.

SH Does that still happen?

SC Yeah, it's a miracle that it is still alive especially with a lot of the theatres shutting down because of lack of funding coming from the government.

SH *A Ridiculous Spectacle in One Act* [by Tomson Highway] came out of some workshops done in 1985. It seems to have different names at different times. Is it the same as *Many-Toe Lynn Aileen* [sounds like Manitoulin Island]?

SC It is the same thing. [She pronounces it. Laughter.]

SH You invited visiting artistic directors but you were really in charge from 1983/1984 until when?

SC Until [in the later 1980s] it went to Wiky [Wikwemikong Unceded Indian Reserve], I guess.

SH Were you pleased with the size of the audiences, their make-up?

SC Yeah, a lot of people came out to see the plays; a lot of people booked them. They all went on tours and they did very well.

SH How did you book them in those days? You called the community centres?

SC Yeah, I called the band offices and found out who was doing cultural events in their communities. I'd call the schools to see if they'd be interested. A lot of organizing went into the tours. It was very time consuming, especially being a volunteer artistic director. I volunteered all those years. I was never paid as an artistic director.

SH Was anybody else paid?

SC Well, yeah, Tomson and Larry and anybody else that we brought in other than myself, there was always a salary to it. Basically it was me and Blake most of the time doing all the paperwork because he was the President too, during all those years, and he put a lot of free time into Debaj as well—posters, organizing fundraising things. We did most of that on our own time.

SH Now, the workshop form of creation—was that always part of the work?

SC Well, when I first started theatre I was workshopping a lot of other people's work as an actor. I thought that was the process. So we just continued doing that process. It didn't work for me as a playwright. I don't do it anymore but I know a lot of companies still do it. But I'm not disregarding the process. Do I need it or don't I need it? That's the process I learned and it worked really well. The only thing that bothered me about this workshopping was that when people workshopped the script they were not given the first refusal to act in the play. If you workshop and develop a character you should be able to perform it.

SH How did you invite these people? You said that Larry Lewis was in charge of workshopping the *Shadow People* script. Did he invite René Highway and Tomson Highway?

SC We talked about actors who would be best suited for these roles, who would be best suited to develop the roles. That's how we cast the workshop. When the time came for the actual play, a lot of them were not available.

SH Tell me about Larry Lewis?

SC Larry Lewis—how do I explain it? He played a major role in the development of Native playwrights and theatre and was a great director for Native actors.

SH He says it was the success of *The Rez Sisters* [by Tomson Highway, first workshopped at De-ba-jeh-mu-jig] that really gave Native theatre a push forward, but he was involved before that?

SC Oh yeah, he was. I mean Native theatre was really not recognized if you weren't in Toronto and we were not in Toronto. People didn't even know we existed for a while. We had already been doing a lot of plays before people realized we were around. It is never ever said—I've never seen anywhere where it says—that *The Rez Sisters* was developed by De-ba-jeh-mu-jig. It always looks like it came out of Toronto and it's not true.

SH *Many-Toe Lynn Aileen* was described as street theatre in the sense that it was just done for the people who came off the Chicheemaun ferry [in South Baymouth].

SC Yeah, it was just one of those "let's do this" things.

SH Did you choose *Ayash* as a script? You were Artistic Director then.

SC I'd done it before, myself. I really liked the story and I decided to do it here for this area.

SH There was that letter in *The Manitoulin Expositor* in 1987 [19 August] in which Sharon Sproule of Espanola stated that she brought some people from the theatre community in southern Ontario to *Ayash* [by Jim Morris, choreographed by René Highway] and they all said that the play was one of the best they'd ever seen, that it was better than anything they saw in Toronto. She was asking why the theatre wasn't packed with people. I guess it's just because there aren't that many people up North?

SC *Ayash* that Debaj had done was the best of all the *Ayash*es that I had done. It was really well done. Larry [Lewis] directed it. That was one of the best shows that I remember from way back in the 1980s. I really enjoyed it. A lot of people enjoyed it and came up to me after the performance to tell me as well.

SH Because the story was so great? It's a Cree legend that's been published.

SC The whole thing, costumes, props, everything put together, the dancing and singing.

SH You kept the admission fee low?

SC We wanted people to come and see it. We didn't want to keep them out. What happened was, the first time we did the show over here a lot of people in the community said they didn't see it because it was too expensive for them. We didn't want to do a show and exclude all the people who couldn't see it. There were a lot of times when I was watching the box office where there were ten kids hanging around outside. I just let them in so that they could see it. You have to do that for some people because you know they can't afford to go in but they should see it.

SH   You did the box office too?

SC   Yeah! [Laughter.]

SH   So you'd write the play and do box office, too. That's unusual. [More laughter.] The idea of the soap opera influenced *Nothing Personal* [by Shirley Cheechoo and Alanis King] in 1988.

SC   Yeah, we tried to figure out how we could do it, experimenting with comedy. We thought that the soap opera might be something interesting.

SH   Were you conscious of wanting to do some plays as comedies and some that were not comedies? Were you thinking about a mix like that?

SC   I mean, with my work and other people's work I just let it go and take it where it's going. I never really wanted to push any direction on any writer. So we just workshopped the piece and saw where it was headed, and if it went toward comedy then we did comedy and if it went serious we went serious. You kind of have to let the storytelling take its own flow. Sometimes when you try and redirect something that you're creating it turns into a disaster.

SH   A lot of theatres, in Toronto for example, would never say that their plays were for kids. I wouldn't say that these early Debaj plays are for children but they include children and involve children in the audience. You wouldn't say that the theatre is entirely for kids but to help young people develop their talent and skills. But the play *Nothing Personal* would be for adults.

SC   Yeah, and so is *Nanabush of the 80s* geared toward a young audience, but not children. When Debaj moved, I went back into the schools and started teaching theatre and drama. The children had been forgotten when West Bay Children's Theatre became Debaj; they kind of just got put aside. So I decided to go back into the schools and start teaching drama again and that's what I've been doing for many years. I go up to Quebec; I go all over now.

SH   Do you do voice and movement and things like that?

SC   I do the whole thing with them, the whole production. I've done many school plays with kids that are like fifteen to twenty minutes long, taking them from auditions to writing their own scripts to directing them and doing their own design working with Blake. Blake comes and helps with the design and stuff. But the kids design their own sets and then we perform the plays for their school and their community. Now the kids that come into the theatre, into the drama workshops, are kids that I pick. I feel that they need some kind of self-esteem, and drama does it. Anything in the arts gives these kids a lot of self-esteem. Teachers will say, "You know this kid doesn't talk at all in school and you should pick this one, and this one's got A's and this one's got that and that and that." Obviously that kid's been worked on and the one who's sitting in the back of the room hasn't been worked on. So I try to pick kids whose self-esteem needs to be developped because I know that once they go through the process a lot of teachers will come up and ask, "How did you get him to talk? So loud? How did you get him to memorize his lines?" The arts are really important for children and they're not taught in the schools.

SH   How do you get them to come to your workshops?

SC   When you tell them that the story is their own story. Say the character is Jack and even though you're putting all your life into Jack, performing Jack, they're actually spilling out all this stuff that they need to spill out. And also there's the fact of treating them all as my friends rather than me as the director and they're just the children. I put them at the same level as I am; I talk to them at the same level. They come to me and tell me things that happened to them last night. And I say that maybe we could include it in the play somehow. And they tell me all the things that they need to get out of their system. They can be bears, and be different animals and different things. The bear can get really angry and I say, "what is this bear angry about?" and they tell me. You get them that way.

SH   So their self-esteem gets built up. The idea of performing and having people applaud must be great for them.

SC   Yeah, even doing the smallest little thing on stage builds up so much of their self-confidence because, really, they just need to be paid attention to. And sometimes academic work wouldn't do it. Most of the kids in my class, their academics are really low. I mean some can't even read; they're Grade 7 and 8 students and they can't read. I help them memorize their lines because they can't read them. Nobody knows that they can't read when they're up on that stage. So they know that there is process to learning and it's not all just academic; they know there is something else beyond looking at classroom material.

SH   How did you get involved in theatre and the arts?

SC   I've always been a performer myself. My parents were very good storytellers and my dad always made us perform things, like he'd identify an animal in Cree and we'd have to perform it. He played fiddle and taught us how to dance. I lived in a very creative environment; my mother was a craftswoman and my dad was into music. It was a performance kind of environment. Then when I got into school I went through the same thing every Native child probably goes through; academics was not my way of learning. I found myself in Grade 9 and thinking, "What did I learn?" I didn't remember anything that I learned. So going into high school and then university, and then discovering that's not where I belong, I went back to the arts. That's where I found myself, too.

SH   In the theatre particularly?

SC   Writing, painting, everything that I've done. That's where I found my self-esteem, too. I learned a lot of it at a school that I went to called Manitou Arts Foundation. Thomas Peltier was the first person who introduced the arts as self esteem development and that was way, way before the Ojibway Cultural Foundation existed. A lot of artists came out of that program and he was the one who really introduced shadow theatre, filming and all those different kinds of ways that we could develop as Native artists. I'd only known this kind of environment existed in the White people. I saw White people movies where I always saw Indians being killed and, well, I didn't want to be Indian, right? [Laughter.] I never really saw the Native art form, like film. I saw the crafts like storytelling and my parents did dancing but he [Thomas Peltier] introduced art that I could use to explore. That's where I started my artistic process: ever since I was a kid, storytelling, the philosophy of life, values, even religion go along with the process. And I know that for a lot of other Native people that I've talked to, the arts are the best way to learn. It's very, very important to listen to the young people. They're going to know what we need to show them. My son is my resource person for the young audience. He's that age.

SH   What years were you at Manitou Arts Foundation?

SC   1971, 1972.

SH   Back to when you did *Nanabush of the 80s* in 1988 written by you, Kennetch Charlette, and Alanis King. You did the music. I guess we think of you more as a visual artist, filmmaker, and writer than a musician.

SC   We were writing a musical play. I was already singing. [She sings.] I thought I could try, I could try a few songs and see how it worked out.

I had to write ten songs; I started writing and putting them to music. Then I showed them the stuff that I was doing and they said, "Yeah, let's use it!"

SH That show [*Nanabush of the 80s*] went to San Francisco for the North American Native Film Festival for the opening night highlight. And then it came back to Cambrian College in Sudbury and had standing ovations and standing-room-only audiences. That's the kind of thing I expect. But to go back to the beginning as we finish up, what made people have the courage and confidence to go ahead with starting a theatre?

SC You don't. It just kind of works its way. I never thought, "Well, I am going to start a theatre!" Not like that; it just sort of builds on its own. You just kind of go along with the journey.

SH Did you ever think that you needed to have a permanent place to perform these plays? Did you ever say, "I wish we didn't have to move from community centres to schools?"

SC Before the company moved I was trying to figure out how I could actually put a building together and to actually have a home for the theatre, to run plays in the summer and also to just have offices, just like the Sudbury Theatre Centre, to have a home like that. Before I could actually get into the process of doing that, the theatre moved to Wiky. I just felt like we knew it was time to let go, let this thing run where it wants to go. It was really the best thing I did for Debaj because then it brought in all this new blood and a new direction. I've seen what they've done and I've liked it. But the whole idea of going on tour—you know the whole mandate of touring to other communities and development of talent—those things they still do. They just have to now concentrate on directors and stage managers and costume designers. They've developed a lot of actors. They're not developing writers; they're bringing writers in from Toronto. We spent a lot of time trying to develop writers at the beginning of Debaj. But they've certainly developed new talent.

SH How did the theatre happen to move to Wiky?

SC I think the community found a home.

SH A building?

SC Because the building here had no washrooms; it was very small. They found a home there and I think Larry said that he was given more support there than he was getting in West Bay. Their board members were coming from that area as well. They don't have a building now; they've moved into a trailer. The other building was demolished, the nursery school.

SH   I'm at the end of my notes. I'm sure there are many things I haven't thought to ask you about.

Tomson Highway

Highway goes on to say that theatre can be an important outlet for Native people who are unemployed and frustrated;
they need an outlet that is emotionally, spiritually, and practically fulfilling. Finding the outlet in theatre and storytelling
is important for them.... [H]e believes that for actors to
develop, scripts must be written to challenge them. Highway
is adamant about the importance of developing new writers.
If Canada is going to have top quality Native theatre, it must
come from the Native writers.

> —Jennifer Preston, "Weesageechak Begins to Dance," 157

As Tomson Highway has observed, "I'm sure some people
went to *Rez* expecting crying and moaning and plenty of
misery, reflecting everything they've heard about or witnessed on reserves. They must have been surprised. All that
humour and love and optimism, plus the positive values
taught by Indian mythology."

> —Denis W. Johnston, "Lines and Circles," 259

— • – • —

*The following interview with Tomson Highway took place 23 August 2001 in
Sudbury, Ontario. Thanks to him and to Raymond Lalonde for giving so generously of their time. Tomson Highway's work with De-ba-jeh-mu-jig
Theatre re-emerged in the summer of 2003 with a new play,* A Trickster Tale, *as the theatre's mainstage production running in July and August. The play
was described on the group's website at the "Summer Mainstage 2003" link as
"a contemporary telling of an age old story" (www.debaj.ca, accessed 26 June
2003).*

*A note of clarification about the very early production history of
Highway's* The Rez Sisters, *quoted from the Acknowledgements section of the
script published in 1988 by Saskatoon's Fifth House: "The Rez Sisters was
workshopped at the De-ba-jeh-mu-jig Theatre Company, West Bay,
Manitoulin Island, Ontario, in February 1986 with Mary Assiniwe, Greta*

Cheechoo, Gloria Eshkibok, Mary Green and Doris Linklater under the direction of Larry Lewis" (x).

— • – • —

SH   Debaj is the longest running Native theatre in North America, it does wonderful work, and yet it's virtually unknown. You were Artistic Director.

TH   I was there for only one year, the winter of 1984/85. First of all, it was very raw. There were no accommodations. I lived in this little camp that was not even winterized, way up in the bush, and then I had to move, basically when winter came. There were no cooking facilities. I had to eat at a restaurant which was like a greasy spoon so it was hamburgers and french fries. I was very unhealthy and I was extremely irritable!

SH   And yet there was such a wonderful group of people gathered there.

TH   I know! There were some fabulous names in spite of the difficult conditions. I had no car and with the salary that I was getting I certainly couldn't afford a car, but when you live out in the countryside you have to have a car. I was hitchhiking around.

SH   How did they convince you to do the job? [Laughter.]

TH   Because at that point I had to get out of Toronto for a while and because I wanted to help. I mean, I'd helped another theatre group in Sioux Lookout before that to the best of my ability and I'm still trying to help out in my own way.

SH   How did things work in those early days? Was everything workshopped?

TH   Everything was workshopped. The one big production that we did was *Shadow People* by Shirley Cheechoo which was extensively workshopped.

SH   How did all of those talented artists converge on the island?

TH   They were mostly from Toronto and they came up very kindly and generously and donated their services when I called them up and asked them—well, donated in the sense that they were paid very small amounts of money. They were wonderful people and we had a wonderful time amongst ourselves. The problem was that I had never run a theatre company before in my life and I guess I was expecting to know everything and I didn't. And you know you just don't go into a brand new job and know everything. There was no funding and no administrator, no bookkeeper, none of that stuff. So, it was like I did it all, everything. I did the fundraising at the beginning. Toward the end half of the year an administrator and a bookkeeper were provided but it was already too late because I had already made so many mistakes. The living conditions eventually drove me out of there. I tried to get a loan from a bank to get a really, really shitty car that a friend of mine had for sale and I couldn't even get that. So eventually I just left.

SH   It's been said that the future of Native theatre depends on Canada Council funding.

TH   I think the future of any theatre in Canada depends on Canada Council funding.

SH   You started *The Rez Sisters* while you were at Debaj.

TH   That's right, and we workshopped it there as well. That was the best workshop, at the very end. The characters were based on my own family, my own aunts, my mother, her younger sister. My mother's name is Pelajia and her second name is Philomena. She had sisters like that.

SH   Do you classify your plays at all in terms of being comic or tragic?

TH   They're tragicomedies.

SH   And they have lots of influences from...

TH   From everything I've read, everything I've seen.

SH   Might Native theatre be closer to traditions of storytelling than to the European/Western formulas?

TH   Well, one of the differences is the coexistence of comedy and tragedy. That's a very large part of it.

SH   I think probably your work is informed by myth and legend that most people like me don't understand.

TH   Well, at the moment there's stuff being written on mythology. You have to pick it up yourself. The books are badly written and there are not that many around but they're coming. People are writing them as we speak.

SH   In other interviews you've seemed optimistic about how Native theatre mirrors both cultures, those moments of magic and transformation. Do you still have that optimism?

TH Oh, I think so. Very much so. We're in the next wave of Native writers and there's a whole bunch of them, whereas back in those days, 1984?, there were maybe two—if that. Now there's a whole industry. But it's still a very small group of people in Native theatre. When you put 150 people into one group for ten years certainly…. Family's hard. I mean, you love your mother but do you want to work with her? For the rest of your life? That kind of dynamic starts happening, and you just need to get out of that and diversify, and work with people outside the community, and that's part of living with the pressures of the environment. It's like asking William Shakespeare to cast only Italians as Romeo and Juliet. It wouldn't get produced! It's like asking only Danish actors to play the role of Hamlet. That kind of thing just isn't good. It's just so narrow.

SH That's very progressive. Is it a popular view?

TH No, but people also don't realize that producers respect that. A Montreal producer or a Toronto producer has actors living within a ten-block radius of the theatre. A Native producer in Toronto or Montreal will not have that so we generally have to fly in actors from Vancouver, from Whitehorse, from Halifax, from Winnipeg, and that's thousands of dollars in plane tickets and then you have to double their salaries, right?, because they're living outside of their own home town. They have to pay for a second place of residence so that basically makes the play impossible to produce. So you've got to give Native writers and Native producers the right to do shows with actors from that area—whoever they are—regardless of race. And so the point is to give those Native plays a chance to fly, use whatever casting is available in that hometown. Otherwise those plays will never get going and you'll have silenced the culture. And on top of that I don't think anyone has the right to go to a producer and tell him or her what to do. It would be like me telling you how to spend your money. A friend of mine directed, a couple of years ago, a production of *The Diary of Anne Frank* with a completely non-Jewish cast, and one of the spots they did on their tour was the Jewish Centre in Toronto, the Jewish Holocaust Museum, and the director said, "Thank God English/Anglo actors and Italian actors are learning what it feels like to be a Jew."

SH Do you see a problem with Native playwrights drawing on the Western tradition?

TH Well, all art is derivative. It's all stemming from something, stories that were passed on. Take the time to study, for years. Learn the techniques. Learn how to write, how to write music, learn how to sing, learn how to act, learn how to paint. It took me years to study that. That's what I went to school for. It doesn't come from the sky. I had to go to university for six years. People wonder why my stuff is the way it is. It's because I went to university for six years. There's only so much you can do with a high school education, you know?

SH   Tell me about Larry Lewis.

TH   He himself had some Native blood in him as he discovered. He fell in love with Native writing and Native storytelling and Native people and eventually moved to Wiky. He lived there for the last seven years of his life. He directed many, many shows. He worked with Debaj after I left. He cared deeply about Native traditions and Native issues and certainly encouraged young writers and young actors from Manitoulin Island. I think what I did was give him a foundation, but he really built the house.

Larry Lewis

(31 January 1954 – 7 June 1995)

> He's like one of the fathers of Native Theatre. He's encour-
> aged all of us, me especially.
>
> —Gloria May Eshkibok

> Without him giving me a chance in the theatre, I wouldn't be
> where I am today. He was the first person who believed in
> me.
>
> —Shirley Cheechoo

> The best man I knew. He let me get away with a lot of things.
> I shall miss him sorely.
>
> —Graham Greene

— • _ • —

*Larry Lewis succeeded Tomson Highway as Artistic Director of De-ba-
jeh-mu-jig, and their collaborative efforts on several of Highway's plays,
particularly* The Rez Sisters *and* Dry Lips Oughta Move to Kapuskasing,
*mark major turning points in Canadian Aboriginal theatre. To quote the
playbill for Centaur Theatre's 1989 production of* The Rez Sisters:

> Larry has been associated with *The Rez Sisters* since 1986 and
> has directed Tomson Highway's highly acclaimed *Aria*. Other
> credits include: *Nanabush of the 80s*, a Native country and
> Western musical; *Ayash*, one of the oldest recorded Ojibway
> legends; his own adaptation of *Wuthering Heights; Jessica**
> [by Maria Campbell, Linda Griffiths, Paul Thompson] for
> Northern Lights Theatre, Edmonton, and *Back to
> Methuselah*, at the Shaw Festival, where he assisted Denise
> Coffey in the direction of this 8-hour epic.

---

* *See* The Book of Jessica: A Theatrical Transformation *by Linda Griffiths and
Maria Campbell (Playwrights Canada Press, 2002).*

The illustrious history of Dry Lips Oughta Move to Kapuskasing *begins with Mr. Lewis having won a Dora Mavor Moore nomination for his direction of the original Theatre Passe Muraille/Native Earth Performing Arts production in 1989 (and the show itself having won four others). He then also directed the National Arts Centre (Ottawa) and Royal Alexandra Theatre (Toronto) productions in 1991.*

Mr. Lewis's other directing while at De-ba-jeh-mu-jig includes several plays by Drew Hayden Taylor—Toronto at Dreamer's Rock (1989); Education is Our Right and The Bootlegger Blues (both in 1990); and Someday, both the 1991 De-ba-jeh-mu-jig and the 1994 Centaur productions—his own New Voices Woman, and Esther Jacko's Lupi, The Great White Wolf, entirely in Ojibway. His administrative talents seem to have matched his artistic and interpersonal brilliance as well, for he applied successfully for grants and otherwise kept the group running efficiently.

But these data fail to describe the man fully. Please see, for example, Audrey Wemigwans's and Rose Marie and Marjorie Trudeau's frequent, warm references to him in their chapters here. Below is a tribute to him written by James Cullingham and published in Aboriginal VOICES *shortly after Mr. Lewis's death, reprinted here with the author's and magazine's permission. (Mr. Cullingham is a documentary filmmaker and coordinator of the Journalism-Broadcast program at Seneca College in Toronto.)*

— • - • —

CAMP BRAGMORE, LAKE MANITOU
MANITOULIN ISLAND, JUNE 11, 1995

Dawn on a grey morning 05:15. Gulls start their crying. Canada geese honk in the mist. A light rain falls at this camp as I write outdoors facing east in the gathering light. There will be no fiery show of a morning sun today.

A great artist was laid to rest yesterday at nearby Wikwemikong. Larry Lewis was 41. He died after a protracted, often agonized, struggle with AIDS. I was lucky to have known him... blessed to have been his friend. Family members, friends and colleagues gathered yesterday at Wiki's Holy [Cross] Mission Church to bid him farewell.

Later as two boys sang sacred drum songs in his honour, a smaller group gathered at his final resting place. Larry Lewis's ashes will be scattered at the edge of a peaceful grove of oak trees with a view of the bay that he loved on a hillside cemetery above Wikwemikong.

During the service the priest said that Larry was "now for the ages." In a humble, moving testimonial, the priest said he'd been in a field in southern France where Van Gogh had painted his "Sunflowers." The priest said that Van Gogh's painting seemed more real to him than the sunflowers themselves. He said that Van Gogh could do this because he was more real than most of us. He had dove in and gathered the essence of those sunflowers. Now they could be shared, enjoyed and admired by people "for the ages." The priest said that Larry Lewis's life was similar. That in a very powerful way his life would continue in the works he created and the people he touched so profoundly. How true.

Larry Lewis gave the end of his life to Native theatre, to friends, to children and to the community of Wikwemikong which embraced him in life and comforted his spirit with its sacred songs at the time of his death.

Through his work with Tomson Highway, Drew Hayden Taylor, Alanis King-Odjig and countless others, Larry Lewis was a linchpin of the movement that brought Native theatre to stages across Canada and beyond in the past decade. It was at Wikwemikong where Larry and a Cree musician/poet with a lightning bolt of theatrical inspiration changed Canadian theatre forever. They worked and played and drank and swore and laughed and smoked and worked and worked and worked and worked and finally brought *The Rez Sisters*, *Dry Lips Oughta Move to Kapuskasing* and the still-to-be-produced *Rose* to life. The collaboration of Tomson Highway and Larry Lewis is truly "for the ages."

It was also at Wikwemikong where Larry helped marshal the extraordinary youthful talents of Wikwemikong as artistic director of De-ba-jeh-mu-jig Theatre Group.

Larry Lewis was the most generous artist I've ever known. He was a faithful listening post, an advisor who understood the difference between facilitation and domination and a no-nonsense bullshit detector. He did not coddle—he pushed really hard when he felt the need. He did not condescend—he challenged people to go within themselves, to retrieve their own truths, to ask the imponderable questions that great writing and acting requires.

Those of us who were fortunate enough to know this kind, brilliant and gentle man have suffered a great loss. As individuals we will grieve him for a long time to come. As a community there is much good to be drawn from his passage through this life.

Larry Lewis was loving. He had a wicked, almost manic sense of humour. He was sensual and incredibly sexy. He was a tireless worker who somehow remained considerate and patient while being a hard-ass all at the same time. He did not judge people by race, age, gender, sexual preference or economic status. He was very much an equal opportunity kind of human being.

Larry Lewis was a White, gay man who ended up the adopted child of an Indian community some 550 kilometres north-west of Queen Street West [Toronto]. He gave much to Wikwemikong. He was given a home in return.

Larry is at rest now in the shade of those oaks overlooking Wikwemikong Bay which he would gaze at every day from his home. As we scattered tobacco there on Saturday, June 10, 1995 I remembered something he'd told me about two years ago. Larry said he'd "finally found a home" at Wikwemikong. He honoured the place and was honoured in return. As each of us paid our respects, stricken with grief and tears, we also know that, like Van Gogh's "Sunflowers," the life and profoundly good work of Larry Lewis will endure.

—Aboriginal VOICES

Larry Lewis, 1954 – 1995

Alanis King

An ideological home provides people with an Indigenous location to begin discourse, to tell stories and to live life on their own terms. An ideological home is a layering of generations of stories, and the culmination of storyteller after storyteller, in a long chain of transmission. To be home… means to dwell in the landscape of the familiar, collective memories…; it involves having a personal sense of dignity.

—Neal McLeod, "Coming Home
Through Stories," *(Ad)dressing our Words*, 19

[T]he idea of working from an Indigenous source through songs, dances and stories reinforces the worldview of a Native performer whose creative starting points would then originate from the land of his or her ancestors…. A main distinction between contemporary Native performance and colonial Western theatre is that the roots of Native performance can be traced to the lands of this country.

—Geraldine Manossa, "The Beginning of Cree
Performance Culture," *(Ad)dressing our Words:
Aboriginal Perspectives on Aboriginal Literatures*, 179–80

— • – • —

On 10 November 2000, Alanis King, former Artistic Director at De-ba-jeh-mu-jig Theatre, and then Artistic Director of Native Earth Performing Arts, spoke to me at the Native Earth offices in Toronto. Her vision of Native theatre is invaluable.

— • – • —

SH   How did you come to be Artistic Director at De-ba-jeh-mu-jig?

AK   I am taking myself back to '86 and I had just come out of the Native Theatre School which is today the Centre for Indigenous Theatre. Shirley Cheechoo called me because she needed an actress in the fall for a De-ba-jeh-mu-jig show, so I went and read in *A Ridiculous Spectacle* by Tomson Highway, and that was directed by Michael Cariauna. What we did at those times.... Blake Debassige was in it, too, and that's Shirley's husband, so we were on tour together and we went as far away as Winaway, Quebec; we went everywhere as well—all over the place. Erin McMurtry was in that company and Alice Panamick and that was her first time doing a show. So after we did that, we next did some writing workshops because Larry Lewis came to town with Kennetch [Charlette] and Shirley Cheechoo, and we wrote *Nanabush of the 80s* and *Nothing Personal*, and then we produced them. Larry Lewis was the Artistic Director and he would make all the applications for funds and he was a Stratford-trained director—and he was a personal and close friend of Tomson Highway.

And I think that when Tomson was Artistic Director at De-ba-jeh-mu-jig he brought in Larry to Manitoulin and he introduced Larry to everybody, and when we did the writing workshops, Larry was there full-time in that two-bedroom house. The first De-ba-jeh-mu-jig Theatre was in West Bay and it was a house owned by Blake Debassige's mother and then she sold it to De-ba-jeh-mu-jig later and it was the operating office. It didn't have a washroom or anything, and Larry would just go over to Blake and Shirley's to use theirs. I think Gloria Eshkibok was also on the Board of Directors, but in '86 it was very exciting because in Toronto, at the same time, Native arts were flourishing with Tomson's work, *The Rez Sisters*, so Larry and Tomson produced that here at Native Earth and then they swooped up Gloria Eshkibok because she was perfect for that part of the Biker chick, Emily Dictionary.

Tomson actually did a lot of that writing on Manitoulin and up until opening night the reserve was going to be called Wikwemikong but Gloria said, "no, I don't want this to be called Wikwemikong!" so they ended up calling it Wasaychigan Hill and the rest is history. But he modelled a lot of those characters after a lot of zany women he met on the island plus his own family. Anyway, Larry nurtured us all to do the play writing because we had no scripts and didn't know what De-ba-jeh-mu-jig was going to produce next. We would write the scripts and act in them and tour them, and now I wonder how many tours I went on at that time. Well, we did quite a few and then in the summertime we tried to do something permanently on Manitoulin so that the tourists could come to us rather than us going out; and we would go out and we would tour schools or community centres and a lot of the centres might not have stages or proper dimensions for the plays so we would have to adapt sometimes if we went to far northern communities, but we would always make do because the show had to go on, and also because for the people who greeted us in those communities it was a first-time experience to see live theatre.

When I look back now… we were packed up doing eighty shows in three months and day after day after day—you know, strike, set up, perform, strike, set up, perform, sleep wherever you can. We did billeting. We never had a hotel room—a hotel room was a big luxury but that came a little later, and then we got invited to the San Francisco Indian film festival through Shirley's connections. They brought down an excerpt from *Nanabush of the 80s*, and that was the first country and western musical, and the premise of that was they got their first major gig to play the Saturday night at the Wiky Pow Wow, so it was a big deal. And after *Nanabush of the 80s*, I'm just trying to recall…. At that time I had been acting in a few shows, so I really wanted to get some training and that's when I auditioned for the National Theatre School, so I went to that school from '89 to '92. When I graduated from there I came back to Wiky and then I was asked by the people there if I would be the Artistic Director, so I said yes.

I had always heard of the Manitoulin Incident as part of Wikwemikong's history and I started to write that play on my own. I started to do a lot of research and I did that at Jesuit College here in Toronto and at other Ontario archives and gathered a whole bunch of information. When I had a draft I also gave it to about four former Chiefs of Wiky to go over it, and then finally we were able to come up with enough funding to produce it—because it was a company of about forty-nine people that first summer, and I was about twenty-eight or something. But we pulled it off and we got tenth-anniversary funding from Canadian Heritage so I guess they were really instrumental in helping us to produce the play. Because it was so successful, and it was directly related to Wikwemikong's history, our own community started to come out in droves and they learned something new about theatre and their own history that they didn't realize, with *The Manitoulin Incident*.

After that we decided to remount it and we thought maybe it could be the *Anne of Green Gables* of Manitoulin, and we could keep it going as an annual thing. Because of lack of funding, it didn't go that route, but we remounted it the second year and added some really interesting design elements including putting the water in there, and making the fish part of the person, rather than a big mass covering their bodies. Other adjustments were made and we went further with it the second year so that was really great. It was a really amazing experience because being outdoors, and creating that gutted-out form of the residential school as our play stage on the ground of where the original incident took place, all led to the total magic realm of it, along with introducing my work. It has always been that we have this spiritual magical element to any of our mythic beings and they could enter any kitchen sink anytime they want to, and we are going to animate them and create them because that's what we believe. Also it is really a theatrical way to tell the story, and it was also part of my belief that if you believe you are a member of a clan then that means that you believe in your spirit and therefore your spirit is all around you. We could share with the audience how our beliefs are shown through our plays and, you know, play out those animals or play out those myths within the realm of reality, of our history—starving, relocating, going through all these other phases.

Nothing Personal was a two-handed gossip play, and it was a comedy based on a welfare worker and a potential welfare recipient. I felt that that really put on display exactly how our own soap opera could be. That's what we were trying to play—we tried to say, "you want to see a soap opera, just come to any reserve and you catch people talking about everyone and no one is spared!" A lot of it's true or it's made up and it becomes believable. That was a real gas to do.

We had some real key audience members during some of those shows. For instance, Lillie Oddie Munroe, Cultural Minister [Ontario Government], came to one performance of *Aria* which was written by Tomson Highway and we did a double bill with *Nothing Personal*. She came there and later on she supported De-ba-jeh-mu-jig's request for a van, so that was kind of good. And then Jan McIntyre, who was at the Ontario Arts Council, had never given us core funding but she came to Wikwemikong finally and saw *Ayash*. We were on tour; we toured to Wiky and we were going to close the show there. The performance was so exciting, and then the lights blew and we had no lights, but we had the gymnasium so we had to use regular flourescent lighting just when the most important audience member, Jan McIntyre, was there. But she saw what we went through so that the show would go on and she was so impressed by all of that—in spite of the lighting. After that I think De-ba-jeh-mu-jig went on to core funding so, you know, it took some people to make their way to our plays before we got that support. Once we got on core funding, after that, you are pretty well monitored by your own peers and then they go up there to see a show and they assess it and send that assessment in to the funders and you keep that going all the time.

So creatively, artistically, I really made my way, you know, to be allowed to create characters, to create stories and especially to create plays that were relative to my life, or my history, or my family's people. Our work revolved around Odawa, Ojibway, and Potowatomi, the Three Fires people, and that is predominantly what Manitoulin Island and the whole surrounding Great Lakes are. That's where we drew a lot of our content from, and whether it was contemporary, or historical, or mythical, the Ojibway language was our determining factor. So one time, for instance, we did *Lupi, The Great White Wolf.* When that was told orally by Esther Jacko on Birch Island the feeling was, "let's make that into a play." But Esther was not going to allow it to be a play until she asked her grandmother's permission, who she had heard the story from, and then her grandmother said, "go ahead and make it into a play if you perform it in the language." So that was a really good kick-start for us, all of us young people, you know, sort of going into our own language and being able to perform it on stage with accuracy so that elders could understand the young people. But that was all the next huge challenge and it was so beautiful to see.

I didn't have a hand in the first *Lupi.* Again, Larry Lewis directed that and it was set outdoors just in the bush that was cleared by Audrey Debassige's dad; he just made that play stage for them and it was beautiful because they had live fires. A lot of things that we were able to do at De-ba-jeh-mu-jig you can't do in the city. You can't put a live fire on stage without getting insurance—you know, all that stuff. There are so many restrictions to creators here in the city but we had free rein there. That was really beautiful and that's what made it unique, I think, a lot of times when outsiders would come and see it because they wouldn't see theatre like that normally, you know—just sort of an open setting like that in the bush. So I think *Lupi* caught some attention. People from the Brooklyn Academy of Music who came to see it then invited it down there. It took a couple of years, but we went to Foreign Affairs for help and with our performance fees we had to raise about $100,000. I took nineteen people from Wiky and two professionals—a co-director and a lighting person—and we all went down to New York City, Philadelphia, and Pittsburgh, and we did *Lupi, The Great White Wolf* all completely in Ojibway.

Once, in Brooklyn, they wanted us to do translations on the side and make English happen during the show but I couldn't really see us sort of re-blocking everything to suit that need, and it seemed to be their artistic people, all the adults, who were pushing for this, and the solution ended up being that Esther Jacko who was on the tour introduced the show in

English but the whole play was performed in Ojibway. We had sound cues and it was to the second, so we couldn't really change a lot just like that upon arrival. I knew that our decision was best when there was an audience of about a thousand Brooklyn kids at the first show—*Lupi*'s cast itself ranged in age from thirteen to seventy-two. The little kids saw it and they were anywhere from six to ten years old. You could swear they understood every word because they were all clapping and they were all cheering and stomping their feet to the music. When the bad wolf would come by they would react to that and then when the hero was in danger they would react to that, so it was just the most amazing experience as an audience member to see those thousand Brooklyn kids enjoy it. They loved it and the house was just riveted, and you should have seen the cast perform that show! They were jumping two feet higher than they usually did and their energy was way up far, and that was nice.

So, I think that *The Manitoulin Incident* really created the profile of De-ba-jeh-mu-jig being professional, and that being our tenth year we had some sort of permanence factor. After that I started to research *The Tommy Prince Story*. Tommy Prince was the most highly decorated soldier in the entire Allied Forces. He was Saulteaux, a brother or sister tribe to the Ojibway if you follow our history. His family ended up being in Manitoba just north of Winnipeg, Broken Head Indian Reserve, so I went there and I met his sister and I researched a lot of other things and I finally wrote *The Tommy Prince Story*. And that was in 1995 that De-ba-jeh-mu-jig produced it—about the time that I was departing and heading out. I haven't since that time been involved in anything creatively there. However, when Audrey Debassige was considering coming in after my turn there, she asked me for a letter of support which I gave her. I thought it would be so nice if De-ba-jeh-mu-jig could always have artistic input from people from Wikwemikong, or other Native artists who could find a way to adapt to Wikwemikong and still take in all the oral tradition that is still flourishing there, and maybe they could find a way to keep coming up with content year after year. That has always been the biggest challenge. How do we nurture new Native playwrights? It's not easy; you have to be really determined. So now I guess that probably is the end of my chapter there.

SH You've been doing a lot of interesting work with the Toronto media since leaving De-ba-jeh-mu-jig.

AK ...I'm also creating my own show. I've written a play. It's called *The Art Show* [Native Earth's mainstage production, February – March 2004] and it's based on the visual artist Daphne Odjig from Wiky. It's a play about bringing her paintings to life. Daphne is about eighty years old and she is retired in B.C., so I really want her to see this play, and it's got to be produced soon. And also she gave me permission to write the play. It reflects her life through her paintings—that's the way I like to think of it. Native Earth is going to help me workshop it for the next two weeks. And then I've also been at Lake of the Woods Ojibway Cultural Centre and Sioux Lookout and other places where they'll have a group of youth who want to create a play, so I do those gigs where you help them get into theatre.

SH   Is the idea then to work with young people? I think De-ba-jeh-mu-jig really emphasizes the idea that it started with young people, that the main idea was to bring young people into theatre.

AK   Well I think that even Native Earth should have an understudy program and an apprentice program. The Centre for Indigenous Theatre that does all the training for actors provides an opportunity once you're eighteen. I think that when these opportunities exist for those under eighteen, then you can get summer funding and all that. But generally speaking, theatre does translate, once they latch onto it, into self-esteem, identity, relationships—you know, all that team building. That's what theatre can create for younger people. In terms of the creativity or the play writing, that is individual by individual in my experience. If a fifteen-year-old writes a powerful scene it doesn't matter what age he or she is—it's just the fact that they have the opportunity to get it out there. So Native Earth, for instance, accepts scripts every year up until June 30th, and it develops them.

SH   Were you responsible for starting to use the ruins* as a performance space at Wiky?

AK   Yes, when I found that story [*The Manitoulin Incident*] from one of the priests in Wiky, Father [Francis] McGee, who was there around that time. It was about '89. It was before I went to school. When we were standing down by the Bay, we looked back and we could see the ruins; that's where all those people had stood when that big boat had come, the same ship with the minister, so I was just looking up and seeing the outdoor amphitheatre potential there. How can we use that? And then we were able to keep going with that dream. We just fulfilled it because we brought in a good team of people who were willing to create something out of nothing. [Laughter.]

---

* *Holy Cross Mission Ruins: see note on page 46.*

SH   How did you do it?

AK   Well, there is a format to achieve production. If you have the script in your hand, then you find a director and get your designers, your design team, and then your stage management team. Eventually you get your actors. In the meantime, you have an administrative support system, so you're costing everything and then you're raising the funds. So, when all that came together I chose the director, the design team and the production team and helped in the casting. Then we just set a schedule and rehearsed every day for four weeks and opened the show. So that is basically how we create a show, you know. It is kind of similar all the time.

When you operate full-time, you produce maybe two months out of twelve and then the other ten you are just doing business to get those two months to be creative. It's quite a commitment. But I think that in Wikwemikong and certainly on Manitoulin they are lucky to have De-ba-jeh-mu-jig. There's 633 communities in Canada. I don't know how many have an Aboriginal theatre, maybe less than thirty—I'm sure of it—and there are only about seventeen or so Aboriginal theatres in Canada. A lot of them are new in the last three years [1998–2000]. A lot of them don't have a permanent office space; they operate out of somebody's house or they get a grant to start all these things. Canada Council has finally recognized the under-resourcing and they are trying to raise the funding. And we'll never be like Stratford. Today Stratford would receive probably about $750,000, and Native Earth and De-ba-jeh-mu-jig would receive less than $70,000 a year. We are not at Stratford's level; we don't have the number of buildings.

But can you imagine if we would have had support since we were allowed to leave the reserves in 1961 and had the right to vote? If a company had started then we might have a theatre. One thing about De-ba-jeh-mu-jig is that it has a small office and the beautiful outdoor play space that could be anywhere in July and August. After that, it's up to our touring or somebody co-producing or whatever the scenario could be when you're in off-season. Where are you going to do your show? That's why it's always touring, which is good, to get out there, you know.

SH   Why is it that De-ba-jeh-mu-jig has survived when some other small theatres have not? Is it the dedication of the people?

AK   I think that people like Marjorie Trudeau are never going to let it die. She became a really close friend to Larry Lewis; in fact, Larry's buried on the family plot of the Trudeaus. From my point of view when Shirley was ready to let it go, it was at that time when Gloria, Rose Marie Trudeau, Larry Lewis, Marjorie Trudeau and I said, "Let's move it to Wiky." So it was kind of like a solution of how we could keep it going, and Shirley was okay with the transfer. It was only forty miles away and then we set up shop in Wiky, and then Larry became sick and eventually died. I was Artistic Director at the time. He had kept it going, then I had kept it going, then Marjorie Trudeau and Audrey Debassige came in after me. You see how it has always been that somebody had the baton and kept it going.

Today I think that Wikwemikong actually embraces De-ba-jeh-mu-jig. Every incoming Chief and Council see De-ba-jeh-mu-jig as part of the community and because Wikwemikong is the biggest community on Manitoulin with 2,500 people living there (but 5,000 on the bandlist)—of the 2,500 living there, half of those are youth—there is a lot of opportunity for kids to have summer jobs there. They look forward to that. The theatre is now introducing short-term training with the Second City stuff, but again it's a way for the younger people to be involved. Who's keeping it going? Audrey and the people she's working with. So, I can't see it ever folding. I think there would be a big public outcry! [Laughter.]

SH Could you identify a De-ba-jeh-mu-jig Theatre production by any certain characteristics? Are there certain things that De-ba-jeh-mu-jig always does? Obviously it does plays in Ojibway—no other theatre in the world does that. Is there anything else that could make you say, "This is what a De-ba-jeh-mu-jig production is"?

AK I think the commonness is the language and the other commonness you might find is the casting. You see a lot of the same actors again and again but also usually there will be Three Fires people; that to me is significant because they are not Shuswap people from B.C. who are in those plays or Haida. It's kind of like the size depends on how ambitious they're going to be. If it's touring it's going to be small. The other thing about it is that there's the professional quality, that standard, that all the theatres are challenged to do.

Here too at Native Earth we have to work as sleek and top quality as possible, even if we don't have the top dollar budget, but there is a way to get there and it all has to do with the director and the writer and the cast and the clicking of all that. There are so many elements that come to make it really, really great. I also think that De-ba-jeh-mu-jig, you know, in terms of big names—we've never had Graham Greene come back but he did do a workshop one time; we've never had Gary Farmer act up there, but I think that maybe at Native Earth we could have those people, for instance, because it's Toronto and maybe we could cater to that opportunity. I would love it. It is hard to bring a big name to De-ba-jeh-mu-jig; that was my experience, anyway. So that was why it didn't matter to me if the big name couldn't come because we've been able to create names; we've been able to create writers, directors.

I was going to say that I always created a play for the Native audience, so if I wrote a play I would hope that the small kids would come, or my parents, or my family or friends. I can honestly say that we wrote those plays for the community. I still do today, and what Paul Thompson [theatre director] often might say is that he thinks that that isn't happening—a lot of the time. Other playwrights—I don't know what they do it for. I'm not too sure. But everything that I've done or been involved with was for a Native audience and if anybody who is non-Native was able to share in that experience, great, but you are going to see our point of view. As a playwright that is what I wanted to express: What was our reaction to our history? What did we feel, think, or have to say? What were we doing? Why do we only hear about one side of many of the historical heroes that I've brought to life? Why do we only hear one voice? How can we give them the voice? To me that represents who your audience is, if you are creating Tommy Prince's voice because you want him to tell all of us what he went through or what happened to him and only he is going to be able to tell his side of the story, if someone like me gives him a chance.

SH   So there are playwrights who don't know who their audience is, according to Paul Thompson?

AK   You can make that mistake. He [Paul Thompson] is just so aware that our audience is Native, I guess that's what he is saying, and then also how rare that is. There are some Native writers who might come into a sort of formula by which you can get accepted by the mainstream, because it is something that they heard before, only you are just Aboriginalizing it or something, you know, and you are just saying, "okay, this is my take on it."

SH   When you take traditional stories and stage them, do you think people might think that Native theatre is just for children?

AK   I don't think so when you talk about the Trickster. The Trickster exists in all of us; it doesn't matter how old or how young you are but everybody has the opportunity to be both good and bad and a lot of us are both, but all of us universally, if we have a good foundation, know that good is what we are supposed to be, even if a lot of us fail at that a lot of times. There are times in your life when you are going to be bad. That is what those legends are. So if you are going to recreate a legend and if you do it with all of the respect that it's due, you're going to be creating something for a universal audience. It doesn't matter if the child sees the skunk animated, the grandma is going to see the skunk being animated and respected based on whatever the skunk is doing in the scene. That kind of thing. I guess we've created a lot of legends for an adult audience as well.

We did *Ayash* and there was some very risqué things in there; for instance, the women in one scene had teeth in their vaginas and that to me wasn't five-year-old content. They didn't even know what a vagina was, I'm sure, but they loved those little boxes! [Much laughter.] I think that it's for everybody—legends are for everybody. I mean, that is your culture and that's where you're supposed to learn your values from. If you are doing that just for children you are missing the population who should benefit from that.

SH I don't understand why De-ba-jeh-mu-jig isn't better known. But maybe if it were better known it would interfere with the quality of the work.

AK When I was there, there was nothing more that I wanted. I wanted De-ba-jeh-mu-jig to be on the world stage. I wanted to be right up there, right out there and also for everyone; anyone who was putting on a prestigious theatre festival, I thought De-ba-jeh-mu-jig and Native theatre should be there in Canada or abroad—anywhere, and that was my goal. I always shot for the best production possible. What are we going to do next? Can we be even better than our last show? Keeping going. I think that that momentum we had was really significant for that, creating awareness....

In 1982 in Peterborough they had the World Indigenous Theatre Gathering—it was called something like that—so I bet everybody was there. Out of that 1982 gathering they said we should create a theatre in Toronto. We should create a permanent one and then Native Earth was created in 1983. At that time, I think Tomson was working in the social service sector; he was like a counsellor. But you know he played the piano, and he was a composer still. Anyway, he came to Native Earth in those years, '85, I think, so he'd come from De-ba-jeh-mu-jig—he was around all that time. But I think that was just the case of Tomson and René and Shirley and Doris Linklater and Muriel Miguel—they were all friends— and then they went up there [Manitoulin] for kind of like a summer workshop experience and then Shirley ended up being asked to form De-ba-jeh-mu-jig. She must've told you about that gathering they had on

Manitoulin, and the Cultural Foundation wanted to have a little play—the Spirit of Sharing Festival. So that's where her own piece first started and then after that the Highways came.

So it's only been since '82. It's only been eighteen years that Aboriginal theatre in Canada has come to be. Of course, you know, it has a longer history. For me it stems from the Lodge, the traditional lodge in our culture, Midiwewin Lodge. When I finally accepted that or maybe discovered that or had that reinforced, was when I saw the Buffalo Dance in the Lodge performed by Dwayne Manitowabi and it was the most theatrical experience that I've ever seen in the lodge. Edna Manitowabi has since— you know, she starred in *Someday*—she was the head woman in the Lodge, she was around that Buffalo Dance inside there. I talked to her about that. She really agrees. We can't say theatre is new when really it's not, but it is in terms of getting funding for it or touring it or creating a production *per se*. But theatricality definitely exists in the traditional lodges today.

SH Storytelling is a different thing. You can tell stories without making them into theatre. There's another step to act it out or tell it to a larger audience. But do you think that in time things will develop along these lines?

AK So long as there are stories to be told there'll always be theatre and probably vice versa, but a lot of stories—people still haven't brought them forward. What I'm finding here as Artistic Director, you know, if we get thirty submissions for new scripts to be developed, some of them might be repetitive in nature, some of them might sound similar, you know, like the city, down and out, drunken Indian survivor turned tradition-embracing-their-original-purpose, that kind of thing. Well, that's not the only story out there but if a writer comes and writes that in a new and original and bold way, that's what makes it exciting to repeat again. I've come to know that there's only like four stories, but everyone keeps doing them over and over again, even Hollywood, and we just keep seeing them again and again. What's unique about us is that we get to add in the magic, we get to add in the myth of coming alive instantly and we believe it, or a dance figure— some sort of spiritual element about it that lifts or elevates it and that's where I always go.

History is another area of interest for me only because I feel, you know, so much of our healing movement is understanding a lot of heroes or creating some sort of significance in the future for the kids to have. That was for me why I wanted to put someone like Tommy Prince on the stage and even Daphne Odjig because a lot of people know of Norval Morriseau and Picasso and people who are also in my play, but Daphne really is the mother of all those people and she can lend a hand there, too. There's so many. And also the women who've been involved. I think that De-ba-jeh-mu-jig has never had a policy unsaid or written but it's always accepted women writers, and if you look at Lenore Keeshig-Tobias and Esther Jacko and myself and other women who've created there, it's been a real nurturing ground in that equal opportunity way, so that much is really, really great.

SH   How did you create the early plays?

AK   Where I started was creating the plays from scratch. We would kind of brainstorm, jam ideas, and then when I took a hand at doing it just for myself and signing my name and creating a play all alone without anybody else being a co-writer, the first thing I chose to do was *If Jesus Met Nanabush*. I wanted to give Nanabush a little voice of what he thought about when Jesus took his place in the hearts and minds of the Ojibway people. I was also pregnant when they were producing it, and I had just had the baby—Dylan was two weeks old—when opening night happened, so I was sort of on edge about a lot of things. But I remember it being so exciting to actually have an audience finally come just to my play, and since that time I've become more and more brave about doing that. I think you know every play is going to have its merit at that time. You could plan to do a lot of really great things, ground-breaking and all that, but in the end you're gonna have the play that you want up there, hopefully, and people will come and they'll respond whatever way, but as long as you've put up there what you intended to, that's all you can really give. After that it's kind of out of your hands. I've always thought, "it's only one play." If this is our process and our experience for this one play, that's fine. We're going to remember that. We're going to do this play and then the next play becomes judged on its own again, so it really went from play to play.

SH   Does the theatre have a copy of *The Tommy Prince Story*?

AK   Probably. At one time I thought it'd be great if they had the fifteenth or so anniversary to publish all of their productions to date.

SH   That would be great. What else do we need to say?

AK   I think I've said it all! [Laughter.]

Audrey Debassige Wemigwans

De-ba-jeh-mu-jig rocks!
>—Jean Yoon, performer and playwright,
> at the Stratford Festival's Celebration of
> Canadian Plays and Playwrights, 2002

Great things can come of dreams, especially when dedication and perseverance join hands with innovation and roots bound deep into the culture of a community. De-ba-jeh-mu-jig Theatre Group grew out of a dream, a concept to bring professional theatre to the youth of the First Nations people of Ontario's North, to provide Native youth with the opportunity to see themselves on the stage, performing works which were born and developed, not out of the dominant middle class white culture, but from their own communities, reflecting their own daily reality as well as echoes from their rich cultural traditions.
>—Michael Erskine,
> "Manitoulin Island is The Natural Destination" 3

— • − • —

Audrey Debassige Wemigwans gave of her time and knowledge at her home in Wikwemikong, Ontario, on 1 August 2002. Thanks to her for the priceless, vivid, engaging detail that follows. And more thanks to her for the many other careful ways in which she helped this book along, too many to list.

— • − • —

AW　I'm not sure how I started in the theatre. I remember I was in college [in Sudbury, Ontario], 1986–88, and at that time they were going to San Francisco, the group, and Shirley gave me a call and said, "Do you have room for us?" I said, "Yes, I can make room." My kids were young so we all fixed up beds on the floor. I think I actually had about nineteen people. You could barely walk around my living room. This was on St. George Street [Sudbury]. So off they went to the airport to San Francisco. That's when they won the Spirit of Sharing Award, I believe.

SH   You were living in Sudbury?

AW   Yes, I was living in Sudbury at the time so it was *Nanabush of the 80s*—that's the one they took to San Francisco.

SH   Who was in that group?

AW   Kenneth Shaw, Alanis King, Shirley Cheechoo, Monty Bass—Monty is the nephew of Will Sampson, the one that played in *One Flew Over the Cookoo's Nest*, the big Indian. Shirley has a lot of connections out in L.A., so he came to work with us too. I knew a little about the theatre back then. I was never really involved in it; I just continued on in school but I met them....

[On meeting Larry Lewis, former Artistic Director at Debaj, now deceased]: Joe [Osawabine, Animator and Artistic Director] and Bruce [Naokwegijig, Animator and Multi-media/Multi-disciplinary Program Manager] and his friends were hanging around at the school when they were doing *Ayash* and Joe said when they were at the school, this man called them to help set up the chairs and they'd get to see the show free. And Joe and I were going to church one day and Gloria [Eshkibok] and Larry Lewis were walking by and Joe goes, "See Mom, there's the man who told us we can come and see the show." And then he comes and introduces himself to me. He says, "Hi, I'm Larry Lewis. You must be Joe's mom." I said, "Yeah, Audrey Debassige." Then Gloria was telling him that Audrey's a friend of hers. And that's how Larry and I first connected; then we started to visit. He told me I was welcome to come with the kids to see the show. I said "okay," so I went to check out the play and I saw the kids setting up so I helped them. So actually Joe and Bruce were the ones to meet Larry Lewis before I did. From there on we ended up becoming friends, Larry and I. He'd come and visit when he'd come into Sudbury. He'd stay with us and he was talking about doing *The Rez Sisters*.

It was one Christmas over here that they were talking about the play, *The Rez Sisters*, and he was sitting there at a get-together at Gloria Eshkibok's where everybody was going for cocktails before they'd go to the dance. Next thing, Rose Marie [Trudeau] is getting ready to go to the dance, you know fixing herself up. I, on the other hand, was telling jokes and when I tell jokes I like to stand up and move my fingers in the air and everything, 'cause that's just the way I talk. People always tease me, "Are you part French or something?" I say, "Yeah, I do have part French in me, my grandpa." Anyway, then I asked Larry if he'd heard how Justine and my brother Sonny built the deck. Justine said, "Yeah, yeah, I built my own deck. Sonny helped me. We needed a level, so I went in the house, came out with a measuring cup half full of water and we levelled every board like that." And right there Larry said, "Wow, I'm sitting right in the middle of *The Rez Sisters*, right here, the very original." At that time they had never found a Native woman to play Annie Cook because they never found a Native woman who spoke so fast and moved so fast and anyways, he phoned Tomson and he told him, "Tomson, you're never going to believe this but I was at a get-together last night and I was just sitting around with all these women who are just like the Rez Sisters. You know they were putting on lipstick and Annie Cook was standing up telling jokes.

Larry was trying to tell me about the characters and I was like, "I'd like to meet this Annie Cook." I thought it was a person they were talking about and he was trying to explain that, no, she's a character in the play. I finally knew what he meant. So the time came when they wanted to produce *The Rez Sisters* so he asked me to read. I said, "Oh no, I'd never go on stage, not me; I'll never do that. I'm too shy." He said, "Come on—just read." You know, he got all of us there; we all did it. I played Annie Cook; Justine Enosse played Pelajia; Rose Marie Trudeau played Philomena and then Gina Simon was there and played Marie-Adele; Gloria Eshkibok was there, and she played Veronique St. Pierre.

Then he goes, "I need an Emily Dictionary." We all looked at each other; we all knew Pokey Fox, and Pokey is always swearing. Rose Marie and I started telling Larry about Pokey—the type of character she is—and he was scared to go and see this woman after that. So he said, "Will you come with me?" So we went over and I knocked on Pokey's door, and I asked, "Pokey, do you want to read a part for a play; we're looking for someone to play?" "Play what?" "Play a character in this play." "I don't act; I don't know how to act." And then Larry was kind of nervous of this woman. Anyways so I just started to read and I got her to read some of the lines from Emily. She said "I talk like this all the time; I don't need no book." Larry's like this: "Wow!, she's perfect for that role." And then she agreed and it was really neat because I was surprised to see Pokey do something like that and she did a really good job by just the way she was too. Her and Rose Marie, they were—I don't know how old they were—but Justine was sixty-three at that time when she did Pelajia, and it was amazing and the cast was right there; it was amazing. We were all, like, typecast for the roles.

SH   That wasn't the original production?

AW   No, the original production was done by Native Earth [Performing Arts, Toronto] and then it was produced by Centaur Theatre [Montreal], and then it was the De-ba-jeh-mu-jig production. Then after that it was done all over, London, Hamilton, etc. Even before we did ours, Rose Marie went to play the bingo girl; she was also the understudy for Veronique St. Pierre at Centaur Theatre. That was one of the things where Larry suggested we come and see the play in Montreal before we got ready for ours. So a few of us hopped in Marjorie Trudeau's vehicle and away we went to Montreal to Centaur Theatre and watched the production; it was really good. Shirley and Gloria were in the cast as well as the late René Highway.

SH   Was René performing?

AW   He was the Nanabush.

SH   And Shirley was...?

AW   She played Marie-Adele. And Anne Anglin played Annie Cook, so I was really anxious to meet Anne Anglin. That's Paul Thompson's wife.

SH   And who directed it?

AW   Larry Lewis did. So I was the first Native woman to play Annie Cook. Then after me, I think Jani Lauzon has played the role and I think Shirley did too at one time.

SH   Is Annie Cook the one who owns the store in the play?

AW   No, Emily Dictionary owns the store. Annie Cook was the one that wanted to go after Fritz the cat. She's crazy about White guys, the bar hopping. She has a big role. She's in every scene.

SH   She has a great scene in the van.

AW   Yeah, the van scene, talking about good old Highway 69 [the infamous two-lane highway that connects Sudbury with the 400 north of Barrie].

SH   Do they sing too?

AW   Yup, her and Emily Dictionary sing a song that Tomson actually wrote for Doris Linklater. One of his loves was Doris Linklater. That's the song he wrote for her, "I'm Thinking of You."

SH   Have you acted since then?

AW After I did that—that's how I got started in the theatre—I went on to do *Word Magic* by Lenore Keeshig-Tobias about a young girl who was stealing and needed attention and was having trouble in school. I remember doing that show and going to Saugeen. School teachers were there from the Native community and the non-Native community and there was this non-Native little girl and she was crying and she wanted to come and hug me, and after she hugged me and left the teacher came up to me and said, "You know she has the same problems you did in the show and it really related to her." As I was walking away, tears were coming down, and I felt related to the characters. It's funny how theatre really affects people. It's a very good learning tool.

At the time that we were doing *Word Magic* we also had two more shows, so we were travelling with three shows altogether all over Ontario and Quebec. We went into Oka too and a month after we finished that show was when the Oka outbreak happened. We had just met those people. The other two shows were *The Thunderbird Children* which was written by Esther Jacko, and *Pictures on the Wall* by Drew [Hayden] Taylor about a young girl who loses her grandfather, and she learns how to relate to the death of her grandfather and how to let him go. So we did those three shows together. We were always changing characters; which show are we doing? Oh, we're doing *Thunderbird Children* for Kindergarten to Grade 2s at 10:00 and then by 1:00 we're doing *Word Magic* for Grade 2s to Grade 4s 'cause that was the level and then for Grades 6 to 8 we'd be doing *Pictures on the Wall* which was about an older girl. So there were three different levels. We'd have to do that; there were times we had to do more. I remember one time we had to do five shows in one day. We did one show in the morning, one in the afternoon and then in the evening the community had us do all three. The changeover wasn't that bad but we'd have like a fifteen-minute break between shows. It was like running an hour and a half with a fifteen-minute break in between to drink water and change our costumes and talk. And it all fit in a big van. So it was really neat.

SH What year was that?

AW 1990. Yeah, in '89 we did *The Rez Sisters* so that was 1990.

SH And after that?

AW In 1991 was when Larry decided to do *Lupi, The Great White Wolf.* Esther [Jacko] came in with a story all written on legal sheets of paper. So he worked at it and transformed it into a script and did all the revisions for the story itself. They just rewrote the story. She just wrote the story of *Lupi, The Great White Wolf* and Larry transformed it into script form. Then he thought, "we need to work with the kids." At this time, I had already shared a house with Larry. We weren't "living together" as Larry was gay, but he wanted me to come and work in West Bay and he said, "I've got a big house; I don't mind the kids. I've always wanted to have a family—this could be the family I never had." He told me, "I'm HIV positive; you know, I just want you to know that right away to help you make your decision." And I said, "Well, it's not like we're going to sleep together; we're just sharing a house and a family." It didn't scare me at all. "We'll be there and it'd be good to support you then in times when you need us." To me I thought it would be good to give him the family he never had, to see what it's like to live with kids. It worked out really, really nice and that's how we ended up doing that. Then we ended up moving the theatre to Wiky 'cause my dad had built a place in Buzwah and he said, "Why don't you guys come home and move to Wiky?" But we left about that time; we were working in West Bay and I think it felt like we weren't getting as much support as we wanted.

SH   Nobody really talks about why you moved over here.

AW   We were just losing too much support. We were just there, you know, me and Larry in the office, and we had Velma Armstrong on staff after a while, so it was just us. Then Winnie Pitawanakwat would come and work and Scan [Clayton Odjig] became our Tour Coordinator and the next thing you know, people that we were trying to get to work were all coming from Wiky. And it was like, "Geez, we're getting a lot of support and more interest and people that want to work with us coming from Wiky." Even *TDR* [*Toronto at Dreamer's Rock*] we did when we were still in West Bay, and our cast members were Herbie Barnes from Toronto, who was originally from Sucker Creek, Puckaney [Jeffrey Eshkawkogan] and Dwayne Manitowabi from Wiky, so it was always Wiky, Wiky, you know? That was pretty interesting. So we did move. My dad asked me to move back home, and we did move to Wiky but we still kept the office in West Bay and we travelled back and forth until one winter we almost got into an accident. That was scary.

   Then finally, Rose Marie was on the Board of Directors; that's how it started. They had just been working on their new building, the Hub Centre [a childcare centre]. We were working out of a house about the size of mine right now. We were in a home with people living downstairs. The first place it was at, was beside Paul's Corner Store in West Bay.

I remember Larry saying that when they had to work there, every time they needed to go to the washroom they had to run to Maggie's Restaurant. So they finally got a house with a washroom, yet it was still somebody's home downstairs. But we worked at an office upstairs and held Board meetings there and then finally when Rose Marie was getting the new Hub Centre the Board proposed that we look into the old nursery school—it has lots of room, we can do rehearsals in there, the little library section can be offices—and so that was looked into and found out that the building was being offered to us! We paid the Band one dollar—you know the dollar thing, how it works, pay the Band a dollar for a lease, more like a donation.

So that's how we ended up moving to Wiky then. It was easy because we had already been living in the community and travelling back and forth. I remember Dixie Rivers Shawanda from Rainbow Lodge [rehabilitation centre] coming in with a cake saying "Welcome." It was really neat. And then people were popping in, you know, "so what does De-ba-jeh-mu-jig do?" And we were getting constant visitors all the time coming in and even volunteering. It was really neat to see that and I thought, "we're really getting a lot of support here." And I thought that was really, really good. I think that's how Mary Lou Manitowabi got started with us; she'd stop in and visit and the next thing you know she got to know Larry, and Larry asked her if she could sew. She said, "yeah, I know how to sew and I have a sewing machine." So when Billy [Shawanda, Animator] came back from the Sault as a designer he was hired on as well to do the *Lupi* costumes. So we did *Lupi*, and we decided to do the first show in the language [Ojibway]. It was transferred into the language by Justine Enosse and Violet Naokwegijig. Bruce's grandmother worked on the translation for *Lupi*. We've had different people work on translations for different shows—Barbara Peltier, Sandra Peltier, Lena White who's passed away now, Sally Atchitawens, and Rosa Pitawanakwat.

So we started doing *Lupi* and the first thing Larry Lewis did was bring Ian Wallace in to work with these little kids and learn about clowns and laughing. Everyone in the *Lupi* cast had to take the workshop. They went to Vinetta Strombergs's cottage in Providence Bay and we locked ourselves there for three days. They took me as the cook, so I had to cook breakfast, lunch and supper for them and they went in and they were all over the place; I looked in and could see people here and people there, and all not talking. I could hear these little sounds. What they'd done is they'd built a mask and they'd put the mask on. They'd look at the face of the mask they'd made first and then they'd put it on and whatever it made them feel, they had to act like that. How would that person in that mask feel if they met up with somebody? So some of them would shy away, some would want to start a conversation or be angry, different things—whatever the mask made them feel. And that's how Joe and Bruce both started.

SH I saw *Lupi* at Sudbury Secondary School.

AW Yes, and we also did it at Science North [Sudbury]. That was done in '91. At that time my dad had the backyard over in Buzwah and he cleared it all up and said, "look at this, you guys; come and take a look at my place; see this, you can do theatre here." So that's where we did *Lupi* for two years and *New Voices Woman*, in the back of my dad's yard. We could fit parking all along the sides. My dad, being a store owner who likes to cook, had corn soup and hot dogs there so he says, "I'll build a little concession over here in this little spot and you guys do the plays over there and in the intermission I'll sell food." And Larry thought the world of my dad, and my dad thought the world of Larry; they just became really good friends and that's the way it went. So my dad was making business at the same time. He never charged De-ba-jeh-mu-jig anything; he was just so anxious to have us come there and make good use of his land.

I remember the year my dad died. He had just turned seventy and we had a big supper. I thought, "I'll make my spaghetti his favourite way this time." Then he gets up and Joe [Osawabine, her son] says, "here, Dad, I know it's Father's Day on Sunday so I'll keep the store for you and here's some tickets for you to go and step dance." My dad was a champion step dancer—he won all over the place with my Uncle Coleman as fiddler, first cousins hanging around in their young days, drinking and partying, you know, step dancing. So they used to win at a lot of places. Oh, my dad was all excited. He got up and did a little jig in the kitchen, and then he goes "Okay, that's it, I'm going to step dance." Then he says, "Well, I'm going to go home and clean up the yard; De-ba-jeh-mu-jig's going to be starting soon." I said, "Dad, relax, we have summer students to help us get it ready; we'll fix it up; you've already donated the land—that's good enough." "No, no, I want to get it all ready." He was so excited back then, you know. So he did a lot of work. That night he went over there and worked on the weeds and that's when he started to feel pains, I guess. I mean we never even knew he had heart problems, and just like that he passed away that night. Driving in his car, he turned into Andy's [grocery store] and he hit one of those poles. They said he went really fast; he had angina.

SH What was his name?

AW David Osawabine. He was an alcoholic and was with Alcoholics Anonymous. They considered him the first Native guy to join AA and start AA groups. You know Bill W, the founder of AA—they call my dad the co-founder because he was the first Native guy to start meetings on various First Nations. My dad joined AA in Scarborough; I keep trying to find an article I know about that was in the *Toronto Star* about 1960, called "One Sober Injun"; I always think I want to write a story about my dad, a book about my dad and use that title. It was a long article with a picture of Mina Atkins who was the writer. Mina's husband was my dad's sponsor in AA, so she wrote about my dad being the first sober Indian who walked through the doors of the Scarborough group and joined AA. He told the police when he was in jail, "this is the last time you'll see me here." He went to Toronto, worked for Manufacturer's Life in Toronto, was the gardener, maintained the land and there he started the group Birds of a Feather.

That was so neat to hear my dad's last message at the celebration of the Birds of a Feather twenty-fifth anniversary. There was a standing ovation when they introduced my dad at that group. There were about 250 people there and he introduced me, and Larry was there and he introduced us—that was really neat. He told the people, "You know I remember sitting here, Parliament Street, in the basement of a church. I'd sit there by myself for a few weeks. Eventually one person started coming, then a few people and next thing you know we had a group of ten people. I was ready to move on. The people knew how to run it now so I could go on. That's when I went back to Wiky. Today I'm proud to see so many people here tonight, 250 people."

SH What is Birds of a Feather?

AW Birds of a Feather is the name of the AA group in Toronto and they run it at the Canadian Native Centre. My father started AA at Gull Bay, Armstrong, Moosonee, Birch Island, West Bay—my dad was all over the place and started AA groups everywhere, wherever he was called. That's a whole other story in itself, eh? We're going off the topic!

SH It's interesting to see what your background is like. You know, to be raised by somebody like that…

AW Yes, he sobered up the year I was born or the year before I was born. By the time I was a year and a half, he didn't want to raise us in the city so he moved my mom and the family back home and he hitchhiked back and forth. He'd come home on weekends to build the house that Sonny's living in [David Osawabine, Jr., Audrey's brother, Animator and Resident Stage

Manager at Debaj]. He hitchhiked to go back to work at Manufacturer's Life, come home on weekends to build the house. He finally got the house done, and he ended up working for CAS [Children's Aid Society], and Rainbow Lodge—he was a Drug and Alcohol Counsellor. He did lots of work there until he retired. Then he started to get into crafts and would travel to Pow Wows to sell crafts. So I never grew up in a home with alcohol and all that. I was really fortunate—a good home.

And my dad was a crazy guy, liked to make people laugh. He was funny; Gordie Odjig had him on interview but he lost the tape before my dad died. He said he and Alanis interviewed my dad; "Oh man, was it ever funny. He'd stand up in the middle of the conversation and do a little jig— 'commercial break,' he'd say, and stuff like that." He was so excited one time—it was the closing of *Lupi*, and my dad put on this great big hat with a feather and great big glasses and a cane and walked in really old. And not telling anybody, not even me, so we're all there at the show. So he comes in, changes his whole character, crouches in like an old man, "*Aahnii, Aahnii.*" And Larry's going like, "who's that man?" I'm like, "I don't know." And then he goes, "*Aahnii*, I'm very happy everybody's showing up here, enjoying this, what these young people are doing here. They're doing lots of good work here." And then he changed to English, and he said, "I just wanted to say thank you very much because you guys brought me business…. I'm selling lots of soup and coffee now," and he made everybody laugh. And then he came back and said, "I just wanted to say thank you to the man who made it possible to do the show back here," and he called Larry up. Larry's like, "Oh my God, he's calling me up," and presented him with a quill box with this great white wolf on it. Everybody stood up for that—it was really neat. So that's the kind of person my dad was.

My parents were foster parents and they had twenty-seven foster children by the time my mother died. I took my foster brothers and went to college in Sudbury. I took Business Admin. I was going for accounting because I love accounting; I was in my glory you know, doing transactions, etc. Nowadays, it's all the push of a button and it's there. So then after that I just ended up going into general business. I thought, "I don't know where I'll go from here." Then I came back home; the kids were upset because I started a placement with the N'Swakamok Native Friendship Centre [Sudbury]. That was my co-op for college, and then after that they asked me to come back for a short term. Then after that they wanted me to stay on and to work with them. And Joe says, "Mom you promised us you'd go back to the reserve once you finished school." So then I thought I'd better go back. And that was right at the time that Larry said, "Why don't you come and work for Debaj?" So then that's what happened. That was in '89. I came and did *The Rez Sisters* and after that I took General Management Training for one year. From there I took Arts Administration in Banff. They sent me and Winnie Pitawanakwat there to Banff for a three-week course. Then from there I went to acting again. Then I came back and Scan [Clayton Odjig] was Tour Coordinator. Then I started as Tour Coordinator when he was on the road. We took turns.

SH　You've been involved now for quite a while.

AW　Yes, probably since 1989 when I did *The Rez Sisters*.

SH　But now you're the Artistic Director.

AW　Yes. What happened there is that I worked with the company. I've seen it when it used to just tour until doing our mainstages. Our mainstage wasn't really a mainstage for *The Rez Sisters*. We performed three shows during Pow Wow weekend and then we toured. I think we did thirty-seven shows all over Ontario from Fort Frances down to Kettle Point, Walpole Island, all over, Kingston, performances in Curve Lake. We were all over the place with that show. Then we did *Lupi, The Great White Wolf* after that. *Lupi* was our first summer mainstage, and our first show in the language. We did *Lupi* for two years and we went touring around and because budgets were low, they brought me along as the cook, me and Rose Marie because Rose Marie had her little girl, Ruby, in the show too. And I think Virginia Shawanda came as another cook too with her girl, Crystal. We went touring and we'd have the propane stove going and we'd cook porridge in the morning for the kids. We'd camp on tour and we'd cook right outside. And Larry thought, for saving money that way, cooking and buying groceries along the way, that helped, and he treated everybody to [Canada's] Wonderland. So we took everybody and I remember taking Justine. Justine [Enosse] was sixty-three years old and I got her to go on the stand up roller coaster! Oh, she had fun—she went on more roller coasters after that, too. She was laughing away and having lots of fun.

SH　She's still here, isn't she?

AW　She's still here; actually she comes out to the shows. We consider her and Eddie King our elders in residence. If we have problems or need something we go to Eddie or Justine. They've always been there for us. I think the last show Justine did was *The Rez Sisters* in 1997 for the Sudbury Theatre Centre and she has done several commissioned shows as well. She does a lot of our commissioned shows for us in the Native language, for Native language conferences. But she's losing her hearing in one ear so she's having a hard time listening to the director and she said, "I don't think I can do this anymore." But she's still up for doing any little things; helping out in language translation. She's pretty good. So that's where the wedding's taking place, at her place [Audrey's wedding in 2002 to Chris Wemigwans, Animator and Training Design and Delivery Program Manager at Debaj].

SH   I guess the big thing now is moving to the new performance space in Manitowaning, having a permanent space there.

AW   Yes. Actually we're going to keep our admin here because we want to be located on the reserve, probably for income tax purposes. So our main administration will be here but I think it's more or less the outreach program that's moving because now—well, we started outreach in 1995— it's grown so much that it's a major part of our company. We moved *The Manitoulin Incident* up to the ruins* [of Holy Cross Mission]. And we've been doing mainstage ever since then. That would have been '94, I guess. I think the boys were probably about sixteen years old, Bruce and Joe, when they started taking improv training and learning to be trainers. By the time they were about eighteen or nineteen years old those guys were out training youth, and so it was like youth training youth in theatre. Bruce just turned twenty-two in January [2002], Joe's twenty-one [in 2002] and they're now designers and directors. That's how these two guys started off as well as Greg and Leroy Peltier.

SH   Greg Fisher?

AW   Yes, Greg Fisher Odjig. I believe he failed a grade just to be in school with these guys. I remember hearing that story, too—here, in elementary school, so he could be with Bruce and Joe.

SH   Do you think you'll keep doing mainstage theatre at the ruins?

AW   I think so, yeah. The Church Council are such great supporters of us being there. Even now, they're having the 150th anniversary for the Church and it's on August 9th or 10th and there's going to be priests and bishops coming to celebrate our Church's anniversary so Garnet Pheasant has us in

---

* *Holy Cross Mission Ruins: Built in 1889 as the Boys' and Priests' Residence for the extensive Holy Cross Mission, the stone structure once also housed a chapel and library. Stone for it was quarried from a nearby island and then carried by hand up the hill from Georgian Bay. A fire in 1954 destroyed all but the three-storied walls and window frames. Forty years later, in 1994, De-ba-jeh-mu-jig began using the ruins for their summer mainstage productions.*

the program. As part of the activities they're going to show the history in the Jennessaux Hall and have videos and old clippings of the Church, how it was before, and then they're going to have a Mass in the Church in the afternoon. I think there's a big potluck feast after and the Council included us. So there's real support from the Church and the Parish Council. They always have supported us and they're really glad that we're making good use of the ruins. It works out for our mainstage, and at the same time we're maintaining and using it. It's really good so we'll probably be there for a long time.

SH The outreach program is really growing though, isn't it? You go into remote communities and develop their theatre artists and practitioners, seek out their resources, and then you bring some of their people to Manitoulin for more intensive training.

AW We've been all over with our outreach program. I know they just did a tour in the St. Paul, Minnesota area and then went up to Winnipeg, and while we were there Chris went and did an introduction to the people out there. We've gotten calls from people interested, now that they know what the outreach program is, and they want us to go and do a week's training. Chris was visiting with one of the guys in Winnipeg and he was like, "Wow, this is great, this is what our kids need up here. There's nothing for them, so…." So it was good sending one of our outreach people out there with the troupe to go and look for new markets. At the same time, we're helping the youth all around Ontario. We've done lots of work in Kenora, Lake of the Woods area. When we went to the East Coast, we offered training out there, too, at the same time as doing our tour.

I'm working on booking the show, *The Dreaming Beauty*, for five weeks in November, and already there's outreach interest at the same time. When I sent my package out for *Dreaming Beauty* we told people about the outreach program. We have our marketing person who's putting all these beautiful packages together and making it really easy for me to talk to people, which is what I'm really good at. I like talking to people; my writing and typing skills are no good. Joe read one of my letters one time and said, "Mom, you write just the way you talk!" So, I enjoy meeting people and talking and selling the show. I'm pretty good at selling.

SH I know, I'm going to talk to Ron about this later, but you're probably involved, too, in the Four Directions method of creation. That's a very interesting thing.

AW I think that started off with *Sky* in 1998. We did *Sky* over here in 1998 and in 1999 we did *Toronto at Dreamer's Rock*. So that's when we brought in Dave Skelton who did his RSVP cycles, which was bringing in the resources: R is for the resources, S is for the score for the show, V is vision and revising everything that they worked with, and P is for performance. And that's the RSVP, and once they did that, that's where starting the Four D creation process came in and was used in *New World Brave*. With the Four D that's for the intellectual, the physical, the emotional, and the spiritual. Alejandro Ronceria from Toronto has worked on the physical, Deanna Sager for emotional, Eddie King for spiritual, and Dave Skelton for intellectual. With *Sky* we did a lot of work bringing it in and I saw them pulling it off in the performance. We had two people—one from Pond Inlet, Nunavit, and one from Iqaluit—and then we had Darryl Bolton from B.C. who's living in Six Nations and was dancing with a troupe out in B.C. We had Peter Tuesday from Lake of the Woods; then we had Bruce and Greg from here, and Tahnee Manitowabi was from here as well. We brought in different cultures, three different ones, from the West, up North and then central, here.

That's where we started doing that, and each participant had to bring in anything that meant anything to them, a picture of their mom or grandma or somebody, or for instance Malaya Kango of Nunavit brought in her sealskin boots because it was her culture, seal was her food. So they each had to bring in two or three items that meant something to them. But they had to talk about each one, what it meant to them, and from there we started to say, "okay, well let's use that, the rope." Maybe somebody brought in a rope because it saved their life one time, or it was used to save some-body in the quicksand... I don't know. That's how things started for the RSVP. And the next thing you know, you see the rope is being used for comedy. That's how they created, from objects, and that's where Ron [Berti, Artistic Producer] and the troupe started to think about the creation process, our spiritual connection, and then brought in Eddie King and Deanna and Alejandro to do that.

SH What else do you need to talk about? When would you say you took over as Associate Artistic Director?

AW I think it was '97. I had left the company to take some fundraising training. I thought this will be good because I love working for the Arts and sometimes you go through difficult times and lots of fundraising's involved. So I took a year off and went and did my fundraising training through the Laurentian program [Laurentian University, Sudbury]—

Resource Development Officer Training—along with Angela Wemigwans and Sam Manitowabi. We worked with the Three Fires Musical Festival as part of our program. It was really interesting to learn about corporate funding and special events coordination, building a volunteer base and how to treat the volunteers. It's like a regular job. Not all volunteers get chosen because it's like applying for a job now to be a volunteer, and appreciating volunteers and how hard it is to come by good volunteers is part of it. So there's all the volunteer training, plus what the Board's role is in the organization and in fundraising because the Board of Directors are asked to help out with fundraising.

So I took a year off to go and do that training and then I came back and I did the fundraising for the company. I ran bingos for a year. I think Ron said I brought in $10,000 that year for the company and it was just fundraising. Then an opening came and it was for the part-time Artistic Director and I thought, well, I have to come up with a five-year plan— I had just learned all that. So I put all that to work, a five-year plan and how I'd like to see the company grow. I remember typing on my computer downstairs when I caught a whiff of Larry's cologne—he used to wear Z44. I thought to myself, "Wow, he's here with me, he's helping me make this plan." I felt so positive; I knew I would get it done. That's what encouraged me. I worked till 5 o'clock in the morning on my proposal, and went for my interview and got the job. It was really neat. I still go to Board meetings and do artistic reports at the same time. I'm sort of like a gopher anywhere. I've always been like that. I've always enjoyed that. I'll go check up on the guys, check in with the box office every day and then I'll take off after the show. I always like to see who comes to the show and greet them—that's what I like.

And one of the big things we always try to teach our people who work in box office and different parts of theatre is the first thing people are going to see is your smile. Smile at people; make them welcome. I know I've been to places where it's, "How many tickets do you want?" It's just a business, but if you start to build relationships with people you'll see them again next year and then they're going to say, "This is our fourth year here." You've got to enjoy, you've got to welcome them; you've got to talk to people. I know we lack that with summer students because we only have them a short while and then they're gone and there's another set of students next year. It's really important to be there to meet people and to talk to people and to see where people are from, what their comments are, how did they like the show.

SH It's great to see you sitting there. Those are your main roles?

AW Yes.

SH For the twentieth anniversary, are you planning to have people come back?

AW I think so, but we're still up in the air about what we want to do. We thought about making ten-minute clips of everything but then that might be too much. And then Ron's thinking, "what about a series of workshops or mask-making taking place for a week? Or having five different workshops happening at the same time?" We're really not sure what we want to do. I want to do everything! That would be a lot of fun. And maybe doing a reading from each script.

SH For people who've followed you, that would be good.

AW I don't know, maybe, just to see what we've done in the past. Or maybe they'll say that sounded like a great show; I wish I could have been there. Maybe it will cause us to remount some of them again. That was neat to remount *Toronto at Dreamer's Rock* for the tenth anniversary. What worked for that was that Drew [Hayden Taylor] had written the sequel.

So Rose Marie was joking around, "Tomson better start writing the sequel to *The Rez Sisters*." But it can't be done because it comes in a series. It started out with *The Rez Sisters*, the seven women and bingo, and the next one was *Dry Lips Oughta to Move to Kapuskasing* which was about the seven men and their game was hockey, but it was the women playing hockey and the men's turn to tell their story. The third production was *Rose*, the musical, telling the story of Rosabella Baez and Emily Dictionary when they went to San Francisco. It was beautiful when they workshopped that play. Rose Marie was in the workshop in Toronto. One of the things that Tomson does is sometimes you have to give your work to non-Native people because otherwise it may never be produced; it may stay dusty on the shelf. So he gave it to the University of Toronto drama students and he told them to get in touch with me. I showed them the little Jennessaux Hall. That's a little bingo hall in this play and today bingo is still played there. In *The Rez Sisters* and *Dry Lips* this place is called Wasaychigan Hill. I took them to Buzwah and introduced them to some Manitowabis—a local name here. And then we had a potluck and did a reading of *The Rez Sisters* for the group—me, Justine, Bertha [Trudeau], Rose Marie and Pokey. At the Hub Centre they, in turn, did a reading of *Rose* and it was a nice exchange and get-together at Marjorie Trudeau's.

SH   Is the Best Medicine Improv troupe still going?

AW   Yes, we had auditions for community members. It was amazing the amount of members that came out.

SH   I didn't know you had auditions for the improv troupe.

AW   We did for *The Best Medicine Show*. I remember Marilyn [Roy] from Buzwah and Karen Pitawanakwat performing on stage. There were so many from the community that I never would have thought would have been interested in this kind of stuff. It was good to see them on stage doing their thing.

SH   You stay in touch with some of the people who worked here, like Alanis King.

AW   Yes, Alanis was here for our opening night and there's quite a few people who still come over. It's really, really good. Leonard Lacquette was with us again which was real nice. He was with us in '92 for *New Voices Woman* and went on the tour for that one, not the mainstage but the tour. The tour was revised down; it was like a cast of seventeen for the mainstage but when it went on the tour it went down to five people. So people had to play multiple roles; it's a lot harder to tour with a lot more people. I think the most we ever toured with was with *Lupi*. *Lupi* had about fourteen of us touring. *The Rez Sisters* just had about eleven of us going, and we had a real house. For the house we'd put four walls together, a roof strong enough to hold us when we'd jump up on the ladder, and our backdrop was painted with big plaque boards, on wheels. When we all got to the Toronto scene, we went "Wow, we're here!" "Bingo!" You know, we'd arrived in Toronto. We got to the boards, turned them around, and you saw the skyline of Toronto. So there we were like, "Wow, we're in Toronto!" It was really neat. So we had to do a lot of our own set up. Actors do a lot of work when they're on tour. We're trying to stick to easier tours. *The Dreaming Beauty* is the dream team. They call that the dream team—it's so easy to set up and it's light and easier to tour. That's one of our things: to take theatre up to where they don't see plays that often.

SH   Do you find you get a good reception?

AW   Oh, yeah! They took *New World Brave* to James Bay on the train and then on small airplanes. It was really neat. Now we're going to go up there and we're going to take *New World Brave* and work with it with the people as well as our outreach program. We're going to stay at Attawapiskat, Kashechewan, Fort Albany and Moose Factory—one week in each place.

I won't be going but I'll be setting up the tour for them to go up there. Now it's a matter of finding how the winter roads are and can we take a vehicle in by train, because I know vehicles do go up by the Polar Bear. We've been all over the place. We've been to Christian Island where our van with all our stuff was on the barge going across to the reserve. So we've had all kinds of different, funny tours. We've been to Temagami—that's another funny one where you have to wait. There's only certain times that you can go to Temagami, Bear Island, because of the weather.

SH So your role is all kinds of different things. Do you still do some fundraising or is that done by the marketing people?

AW I think more of foundations now. Joahnna [Berti, Outreach and Training Director] does a lot of proposals for foundations. We just sat down the other day and did strategic planning for the year and it was the same thing as last year—I found that there is no time left. So much activity is going on. Take for instance, two weeks ago, when the guys were in Minnesota—they had to go to Minnesota and then go up to Winnipeg for a tour while we had *The Dreaming Beauty* there. Chris accompanied them while promoting the outreach program, and over here in Anderson Lake, Tammy [Manitowabi, Youth Programming Director] and Raistlen Jones were doing a weekend camp of working with the youth from the north shore area. It was about youth and leadership. While they were there, Bruce and Cameron [Courtorielle], Joahnna, and Bill [Shawanda] were in Summer Beaver. So, we had like three projects going at the same time. When people get back there's still work to be done—special events, fundraising, bingos with three $1,000 pots at $25 per entry pack.

Again with the bingos here, we started off doing really well, but then there's many organizations in the community that do bingos too, such as hockey teams, nursing homes, churches and it became so regular that we weren't getting the crowds, and at the same time there are so many organizations fundraising it's hard to have people spread their bingo money throughout the whole week. Sometimes we'd work four hours and we'd be in the hole or only make $200, so bingo sort of died down for us. It's hard to find different ways to fundraise. We keep talking about it. So, ideas have come but now it's the time that we're into our mainstage and we're just so busy, especially now that the outreach program has really picked up a lot. We're really, really busy.

SH You have grants this year from the Trillium Foundation, Industry Canada…

AW   We just got Annette [Peltier], Marketing Director, on a large grant to come in and work with us; she's great with computer graphics and marketing. She purchased a computer through FedNor to do our marketing. It's so good to have a marketing person come in to do all that. Last year I was doing promotion and the poster distribution and programs. I'd be out there doing all the work and the press releases; Joahnna would help me with the press releases 'cause my English was never that good; but it was good to get the word out and get the promotion out there. So this year it's been really, really good to have someone just in that field and she's amazing. She came up with all these ideas; we've done postcards before but she used this logo and we got the approval from Daphne [Odjig] to use the logo even on our merchandise—you know our sweaters with our logo on there.

So there's very good support from Daphne. I'm really happy and I was really excited talking to her. She's such a wonderful woman to talk to. You know she tells me, "Well I'm sorry I can't make it down [for the opening], but you tell the guys to have a smash!" It was so cool. I loved that. There was a series of ten of her books that we had to read in elementary school and there were questions that we had to answer. It was really, really neat. So, we gave Daphne a call and we had her permission to produce them ["Legends of Nanabush" as retold and illustrated by her] for this year's summer mainstage [*Ever! That Nanabush!*]. It's just too bad she couldn't come down. She's eighty-three years old now, so it's harder for her to travel. We're sending off a book now for her to autograph so we can sell it off in a raffle.

SH   Is she living in Toronto?

AW   No, she's in Penticton, B.C., but her family comes from Wiky, a big family. Her father married a war bride, brought her home from England, I believe. He brought her home and they had four kids: there was Winnie, Stanley, Scottie and Daphne. Then when she passed away he remarried—Lucy Odjig—and they had eleven more kids.

SH   She had two brothers, one sister, and eleven half-brothers and sisters.

AW   From the second marriage, yes. Yeah, most of them are living around here, in Wiky. Winnie I think is out West and Stanley I think is in Sault Ste. Marie. Most of her family from here are all pretty involved with Debaj—Stan, Rose Marie, Gordie, Greg, Fuddy, Jonathan…

Rose Marie and Marjorie Trudeau

(Board Members)

> Storytelling… is what allows an individual to create his or her personal identity and what permits a society to develop its communal story.
>
> —Irene Maria F. Blayer and Monica Sanchez,
> Preface, *Storytelling*, xi

> This has permitted us to conceive of narratives as actual places to visit, and I have suggested ways to bring back mental souvenirs of our adventures. My hope was to expand the experience from an intellectual exercise into virtual reality.
>
> —Kay Stone, "Stones on the Mountain," *Storytelling*, 11

> Listeners seem to experience the story with remarkable immediacy, engaging in the story's plot and with the story's characters, and they may enter an altered state of consciousness.
>
> —Brian W. Sturm, "Lost in a Story: Modelling Storytelling and Storylistening," *Storytelling*, 15

— • — • —

The Trudeaus welcomed me into Marjorie Trudeau's home at Wikwemikong on 1 August 2002, where we sat in the kitchen during this interview. The home offers a good view of one of the beautiful large bays on which the reserve is located.

Marjorie Trudeau is the current President of the Board of Directors of De-ba-jeh-mu-jig, and Rose Marie Trudeau is Past President. Marjorie graciously loaned her scrapbooks and photo albums containing stories about Larry Lewis.

— • — • —

SH I think it's interesting to have a theatre in the community where people can come and get involved. They can be trained. It's unusual with the mainstream theatre being much more controlled by business interests. This has got a totally different role in the community.

RMT An example is Tammy Manitowabi. She was hired to work with the kids during the day in the community and then she goes and does the show at night. She has a summer program with children up to twelve years old where they come and do improv.

SH Don't you think it makes Wiky kind of special compared to places that don't have theatre?

RMT I really think so. There are people that are very supportive in the community and then there are those who think we're just wasting our time. Their perception of theatre is not the way it is with us or with some other people. But the majority of people support De-ba-jeh-mu-jig; there may be a few that are really against it.

SH And they're against it just because they think it's a waste of time?

RMT They think it's a waste of time but they've never come to see it.

SH There is amazing talent that comes from here.

RMT Yeah, well as young children we used to go out and play and act in the bush. We used to walk around in high heels and dresses. We had a big rock that used to be our favourite place to stand on to sing or act.

SH So there was acting in Wiky before the theatre group?

RMT It was fun. In our home there were French doors between the dining room and the living room and we would put up a curtain. We would make up our own plays and open up our curtain and would begin, and my mom would have to come and watch us and be our audience. [Laughter.] I was watching a program where they were interviewing Gregory Peck and he was talking about movies and acting. He was asked, "What do you think is the most important thing about being an actor?" He said, "I'm a storyteller; when I go up there I'm telling a story and I put myself into that role."

SH I've been thinking about that. I'm surprised we don't talk about that more, even in my own field. I teach English literature and that's really all it is—storytelling.

RMT That's exactly what De-ba-jeh-mu-jig means—"people who tell stories"—people who tell how it was. A lot of the things that we bring out, there are truths in them, things that have happened. I wouldn't say all of it is true but *The Manitoulin Incident* [by Alanis King] for example, was one true historical event.

SH   Yes, because if you don't tell the stories, then they die.

RMT   Another one was called *Someday* [by Drew Hayden Taylor] about children that were taken off the reserves and adopted out because their homes were not suitable. To us they were suitable because we all lived in small houses with maybe one big upstairs with three or four beds. Anyway, that was quite a big issue with so many children being adopted out.

SH   It seems such an obvious thing that there would be a theatre on a reserve that would tell stories, and that people would come and they'd learn the stories—not just traditional stories, but also historical stories or just stories that should be told that otherwise are either going to be forgotten or ignored. Yet no one else is really doing it. Well now with you touring and giving workshops maybe there will be more. Is that kind of the goal, that theatre might become something that develops in other communities?

RMT   I think some communities are actually starting their own type of activities too. I think they're getting to know more and more about obtaining funding to start their own projects. That's what it sounds like from reports we've received. We had a visitor at one of our shows, Lieutenant Governor Jackman at the time. He came here with his entourage to see one of our shows, *The Manitoulin Incident*. I think Alanis was the Director then, and she had sent out a lot of invitations. He also attended when we presented *Tommy Prince* in Toronto at Tarragon Theatre.

SH   I wish there was more of an audience, even from people in Sudbury, because they see the whole culture and everything in a different way when they attend.

RMT   At the very beginning, it was Shirley Cheechoo who actually started the theatre group back in 1984. She's not directly involved any more, but her interest is still there. We always make sure she knows what's going on. She came on opening night; she had to leave the next day to go down to Toronto to the Film School. She did a film called "Bearwalker"; it was made on the Island and it's been on television....

There was a really nice article about our past Artistic Director, Larry Lewis, who passed away. He is buried here, even though he's non-Native.

He's buried in Marjorie's family's plot. He was kind of adopted into the family. He'd been invited to represent Marjorie's brother, on November 1st, All Saint's Day, and he had been honoured to do that. He was just a theatre guy who came to the Island and met everybody and got involved. He got stuck here and couldn't go back to the big city. He had a real drive and encouraged people not to give up. He was always involved in fundraising and cleaning. For the fundraising they went all over and asked for donations and then played bingo for donations as prizes.

He really kept us going. He was the one who really got it started in Wiky when we moved over here and Shirley just kind of left it up to us. And that old building, the nursery school, has been torn down now. It was a school, a nursing home, then a nursery school, and as a Debaj board member it was my duty to ask for that building. We got to use it for a dollar a year since 1990. It was torn down in 2000 because it was condemned.

SH Was there no space here on Wiky?

RMT There was none. There was the old community hall that we tried to get next. We made our request but it was given to Daystar [religious organization]. So we didn't have a place. We even rented out of South Baymouth for a while. We're a little closer now and everything's been moved to our new space at Mastin's [in Manitowaning]. Now the only real indoor space is the trailer used for office space. We use Jennessaux Hall for the props. It used to be a little chapel.

It's good to have Ron [Berti] on board. We know that Audrey did her best and Alanis, she's going in a different direction for herself. When Ron came on board, we felt that commitment from him as well when we interviewed him. We believe we got the right person. He's very much like Larry in his commitment; he wants the theatre to succeed. He's one of those guys that will work for hours and hours and get things done. He's got his wife [Joahnna] helping him and it's good to have people on board like that.

SH Most theatres need that core of people that are really dedicated. It's a hard time for the theatre right now but it's certainly worth all of the effort.

RMT Yes, and we have made changes, like he's Artistic Producer and that's his title. He came to the Board with his ideas and we approved them. Even at our last Board meeting he told us that he will be giving more responsibilities to those who are on staff, giving them titles that will make them feel that they are in charge of certain areas and they will take on that responsibility. I think that's a good idea.

SH He probably feels that he's developing a core group of people that know what they're doing and that have a good vision and are hard workers. That's so important because you can't rely on one person. It's very hard to replace that one person. Do you think the theatre will go back to doing a script, like Alanis's *The Tommy Prince Story*, if you start to get them again? Now, Ron and Audrey are doing traditional stories or ones that the actors have improvised.

RMT I think they will because that is one of the responsibilities of the actors themselves. We do get scripts sent to us and the actors review them. They had a workshop type thing where they reviewed so many scripts that had been sent in. They pick what they want to do. We do get scripts in. Drew has a new one that he's trying to get in. I'd like to see another one of his. We were actually the first ones to put some of his work on stage, such as *Toronto at Dreamer's Rock*, when Larry was helping him during the writing of the play.

SH He says he learned to do theatre here with Larry Lewis.

RMT He learned a lot with Larry. I think there's a lot of people that did get a lot of inspiration from being here.

SH It's kind of a special place here, something about the air. It makes you want to live here.

RMT It's like the Spirit is here. That's why it's called "God's Country." One year when we first got the dockslips in, we had the van pick people up at the docks and bring them in to the show at the ruins and then take them back down to their boats. That was interesting.

SH That reminds me of a play I actually saw in the water down here.

RMT I forget the name of that one; that was fun. Gloria was in that one. There was another one, *Lysistrata*. That was totally fun! We actually marched from the old theatre building down to the beach and started doing that, sort of advertising as we go along. I was in that one, and Rosa Pitawanakwat. Lima Jacko and Annie Pangowish (Tabachek) were playing their fiddles on the water. Plus there was another one with Jeffery Eshkawkogan. He started back in '84 acting right here; I don't remember what they did—*The Jukebox Lady*, I think. It was one that Shirley produced.

SH   I spoke to Tomson Highway a year ago, I guess.

RMT   Tomson's another one who just loves to continue things. He was here last fall before he went to France, cooked up a chicken dinner. Was it ever good, too. We all had seconds. I don't think Tomson is finished with *The Rez Sisters*. I said, "when I see that Tomson, I'm going to tell him to make that into a movie, and I'm going to be in it!" Can you imagine if *The Rez Sisters* was made into a movie? It would be a comedy type thing.

SH   It should be a movie; now that you mention it, I'm surprised it hasn't been. Well, he still has the idea that it's going to be a seven-play series, isn't it?

RMT   He was trying to do another one: there was *The Rez Sisters*, there was *Dry Lips*, and *Rose*. I went when he workshopped it [*Rose*] and I did one of the readings; then we went to watch the rough—it was about four hours. Paul Thompson was directing it in Toronto. But the singing was just beautiful.

SH   Tomson and Patricia Cano did part of it last year in Sudbury and the music was so beautiful.

RMT   Didn't the University of Toronto do it as well?

SH   Yes, I missed it, but they did the whole thing. It sold out very quickly.

RMT   I went to that, too. The kids were really into it. They came here and we read to them, and then they read *Rose* that they were going to do.

SH   I guess the reason it doesn't get produced is that the cast is really big and they've got motorcycles coming on stage.

RMT   They did have a motorcycle.

SH   I love the improv that I've seen here and I also love the completed scripts that people send in. I'm sure you'll probably have a little bit of both in the years ahead. Do you think that it's kind of going back to theatre for young people? It started out that way and the last few such as *The Dreaming Beauty*, *New World Brave*, and *Ever! That Nanabush!*—anybody can enjoy them but they seem to be more…

RMT   Maybe more family orientated, so parents can take their children.

SH   Maybe, but that's not a decision of the Board is it, to go back?

RMT   No. They're very creative people; they do it all.

SH As long as they're growing and doing a good job, then you sort of don't get involved?

RMT No.

SH I'm supposed to stop by the office to pick up all the newspaper clippings from '99 through now, but that wouldn't have anything about Larry Lewis.

MT You can borrow this. [She offers her scrapbooks and photo albums.]

SH Maybe just to get a sense of his life because I really don't know anything about him.

RMT Audrey has given a lot. She has worn many hats here and has done a lot.... We usually meet together at different places. We move around to different Board members' houses. So it's like a get-together at the same time as we do business. And if we can't meet, then Ron will just phone each Board member and ask what they think. Not everything has to go through the Board as a motion.

SH You don't have a set term? You're just kind of on the Board until you don't want to be on it anymore?

RMT Yes, I was the President for twelve years. And then Marjorie stepped in. I know that with some places the term is two or three years long, for example. I was on the Board of Governors at Cambrian College [Sudbury] and after two terms, six years, I had to step down. That was interesting. I got in there through my boss's recommendation from the Board of Education. I did have to write my letter of interest and the next thing I knew I was accepted to be on the Board of Governors. It was a learning experience because at the time they were building the Learning Centre and Norcat. It was a learning experience even though I didn't say too much. There were all these executives there so I didn't want to say too much; I was there more or less representing the Natives. So I was there six years. And they don't pay an honorarium. All they paid was my mileage, and then I'd have to take a day off to go to these meetings. I'd use up my own leave.

SH Are you a teacher?

RMT I'm Program Manager of a multipurpose childcare centre here at Wiky for the past twelve years and in childcare for a total of thirty years. We're under the Board of Education because we have a nursery school and a daycare program at the centre. We used to be under the Band but we were shifted over in 1987. Marjorie's a teacher.

MT　Yes, a Grade 4 teacher. I started in the nursery in 1971 in the old building that got demolished.

SH　So did you teach these stories [Daphne Odjig's, for example, the models for *Ever! That Nanabush!*] to your students and did you also study them when you were in school?

MT　Oh yes, when we were going to school we learned about them. But they're still in the school and they're still used in teaching.

SH　Are they in English?

MT　Yes, the kids read them in English, the Nanabush stories.

SH　Would they read those in the grade schools in Sudbury?

MT　They might if they have language programs or are studying about that.

Ron Berti

Ron Berti, current Artistic Producer, arrived at Marjorie Trudeau's house and joined in the conversation. It has been under Ron Berti's direction that the theatre has developed a creation process so unique that it has won the theatre generous funding, including the means to develop a permanent rehearsal, training, and production space in Manitowaning, minutes from Wikwemikong. His encouragement in the making of this book has been essential.

— • – • —

SH   The Board members mentioned an award that you'd know the name of, that Debaj won recently. Or was it you who won it?

RB   The company has won several awards in the last few years. The Board members might be referring to the Victor C. Polley Scholarship Award which was presented to me in December 1995 "For Outstanding Ability and Dedication in Arts Administration."

SH   Is it an Ontario thing?

RB   Yes it is. There are a few others as well: The 1998–99 James Buller Award for Aboriginal Theatre Excellence was presented to De-ba-jeh-mu-jig in the category of the Advancement of Aboriginal Theatre, The Waubetek Business Merit Award 1999–2000, and the Ontario Trillium Foundation Recognition Award 2002—Great Grants/Great Results recognizing the Outreach Program serving isolated and remote communities. The role of awards in the company history tells us as much about the sector as a whole as it does about our own organization and artists. The first ten years, the awards were mainstream awards—Dora Mavor Moore nomination for director Larry E. Lewis, Chalmers Award for playwright Drew Hayden Taylor, San Francisco Spirit of the Festival Award under the artistic direction of Shirley Cheechoo. I believe this reflected the newness of the work, of these people, of these stories and honoured the ground-breaking contributions being made to Canadian theatre. For the last ten years, recognition has been coming from a community perspective. This reflects a growing understanding, appreciation and support for Native theatre from within the Native community itself, an important indication of the growth in the entire Aboriginal arts sector. Access to mainstream award recognition requires that you perform your work in Toronto, and since this is not necessarily a priority of our company, we have established our own awards which are themselves significant to the recipients. We have the Larry E. Lewis Memorial Award for Outstanding Personal Achievement in the area of Performance, the Tony Wemigwans Memorial Award for Significant Contributions in the Area of Production, and the April Manitowabi Memorial Award that recognizes Youth Commitment to the Performing Arts.... How was last night's performance [of *Ever! That Nanabush!*]?

SH   It was great. The second to last story was all about bad weather.

RB   The thunder and the sun, yeah, having an argument.

SH   Suddenly there was lightning in the background [at the ruins, an open-air theatre] and people were wondering, "How are they doing that?" Then there was rain and the director, Bruce, was standing behind us and I thought, "he's spraying us." [Laughter.]

RB   There have been some great experiences like that over the years, during these outdoor performances. I know it happened in Buzwah when they were performing out there at different times, and it's great when that happens, or suddenly there's a shooting star at just the right time, or a full moon rising over the stone ruins. Opening night there was an eagle flying around for the show. That has got to be a sign that it is going to be a great show, adding a spiritual dimension to the experience.

SH   Sounds like opening night was a big success, and all the right people came.

RB   Yes. It was packed and it was a great night. Although when I was talking with the stage manager last night, Sunny [David] Osawabine, I was concerned about the bad weather we were having in South Baymouth, and I was thinking, "At what point are they going to have to call the show off over in Wiky?" We are only twenty minutes away but because we are on an Island, the weather is very localized. He said it was a great audience last night, in terms of their relationship to the actors.

SH   The kids were enjoying it and I was laughing a lot along with some other adults.

RB   Shirley [Cheechoo] and Blake [Debassige] were laughing through-out the show.

SH   There were a couple of people from Sudbury there but I'm always disappointed that there are not more people, but I guess they don't know about it or whatever. Because it's not that far. People I ran into there were actually staying at Manitowaning Lodge. I guess that is part of their holiday. But I thought it was great. Joe and Bruce were pretty young when I first met them. To think of them sort of running this, I'm very impressed.

RB   Yes, and I think one of the reasons that this happened is that there are other artists out there in the theatre sector who experience long spaces between jobs. But these guys, they're working. Like we had seventy-six weeks of programming last year—and these guys are involved, you know, throughout the whole year, if not creating and performing, then delivering training and workshops. So the amount of experience they're accumulating by working this way where you have a sort of rep company is huge compared to those sitting and waiting and waiting until they finally get cast in a role. They have also had a lot more input than other artists normally would, for years now, and this was finally the time to let them take it over.

SH   So they're like experts even though they're…

RB   Even though they are relatively young, yeah. And I think they made this commitment to theatre at a very young age compared to other people.

SH   And they're able to stay home, and I guess to be working full-time.

RB   Yes, they are full-time, but they are also on the road a lot touring throughout the year.

SH   That's great. Well, we've talked a lot today about the outreach and how successful that is. So I guess there's success in getting grants for it; it seems to be working.

RB   Yes, there are some great examples, great case studies such as the community of Summer Beaver/Nibinamik, a fly-in community five hours north of Thunder Bay, very remote. Joahnna [Berti] is our Outreach Program Director; she'd go out first to do some groundwork, assess how the community is doing, what the local priorities are in terms of development, where the power is in the community—is it with the school Board, is it with the Band Office? She would figure out the lay of the land and try to make some connections, build some relationships, and identify local artists or possible community animators to facilitate activity. Basically, it's all arts infrastructure development. Then our artists would visit the community and deliver introductory workshops—self-expression—and then go back again and deliver a full training residency with a public performance at the end. While we are in the community, we identify the established and emerging artists. For example, Moses Beaver is an accomplished visual artist and musician. We have been able to support him by organizing opportunities to network outside of his community. We also invite emerging young artists to participate in our six-week summer training intensive where they can experience a professional theatre company in full production mounting a new production. We will have a group of emerging artists coming from the James Bay coastal communities in northern Ontario next summer [2003]. We have already made several trips to these communities. We understand the importance of making a commitment to communities for a period of two–three years at least.

SH   So the purpose is to allow their artists to be able to do their work, but also I guess for the networking and also.... Why do you think people would want to do theatre in those communities?

RB   That is not the question the remote communities are asking themselves. They are asking: how can we create a healthier community? how can we support and guide our youth? how can we maintain our culture, our language, our stories? how can we heal from the past, and what is the next best step? Our role is to support those in the community who believe that the arts may be the answer to some of these challenges. I think the youth, the seventh generation, are anxious to find their voice: they need to have the confidence to speak in front of other people. They need a safe forum for civic engagement, and the arts are one way of accomplishing this. You know the size of the youth population is so huge; the largest percentage [of the Native population] is youth. In some communities, 75% of the population is under the age of 25! And you can't really discuss the development of the artists without discussing the development of the community. These must be nurtured and supported together, to maintain and strengthen the relationship between the two, not to erode it and break the connection. If the artistic expression is going to be meaningful to the community, it has to be relevant to the community. So, it's part of what we are funded to do, to help open up these communities and to identify the artists, to teach them how to access the funding that other Canadians are receiving, and also for us to have a chance to work with other Aboriginal cultures within Canada. But it's amazing how much the local context, the community itself, the geography, the local history, the weather, the amount of infrastructure—these affect everything. It's right through to how the people express themselves in their art. I think that is what our trainers find fascinating about delivering residencies; discovering what is unique about each community and identifying where the creative impulses are coming from.

SH   It affects their voice.

RB   Yes, and it builds self-esteem. We are talking about individual and community identity.

SH   But I guess someone who's trained in theatre would then ask next, "well what about the artistic quality of the work?" So you're trying to get them to develop their skills as artists at the same time as they tell a story. It's almost like two different things. It's one thing to be a good performer and to know about lighting and all that, and it's another to have an important story to tell. So you're doing both at the same time?

RB   Ahh, you have hit the nail on the head. Do you see how that concept is a reflection of mainstream cultural and social values? The idea that the story and the storyteller are separate entities operating in isolation of each other reflects mainstream values and Western theatrical conventions. Placing the emphasis on the relationship between the story and the storyteller reflects an Aboriginal world view—whereby all things are connected and therefore have a relationship with all other things. Traditional storytelling is the foundation of Native theatre and is an oral art form, with stories passed down by the telling of them; the storyteller is naturally re-interpreting the stories. They are coloured by their own life experiences, and they are expressed in a fashion that acknowledges the specific group of listeners involved. Recording traditional stories locks the stories into a specific time and place. To keep the stories alive and relevant, we must focus on the development of storytellers. That is the vision behind the outreach program. It is our responsibility to encourage and nurture all kinds of storytellers, from aspiring filmmakers to singer/songwriters. The medium and the style will vary, but the understanding that the connecting point, with the culture and tradition, is oral storytelling is fundamental.

Oral storytelling is not given the respect it deserves by mainstream society. Western thought has invested all of its beliefs in the concept that the opposite of literacy is illiteracy. Literacy is valued; illiteracy is demonized. If, instead, one considers that the opposite of literacy is orality, with distinct ways of thinking and learning and living in the world, but equally legitimate, then there may be hope for the reclamation and validation of an art form that continues to play an important role in many cultures around the world.

SH   We talked a little bit about the method of creation. Do the young people use that in the outreach program? Is that the same?

RB   Well, actually you know the Four Directions creation process, apart from being a culturally and socially specific method for creating new works, has also become a core principle that applies to everything the company is engaged in. It requires that we adopt a holistic approach to all things, and acknowledge the importance of the relationship between, and the association with each other. It means we recognize that we create with our entire selves—our emotional, our physical, our intellectual, and our spiritual selves. So if you create with your entire being, then you have to accept and support everything that comes with the artist. You can't say, "Leave your personal life at home and just access that other part of you and create with that." How can we create with just a part of ourselves? That is why we say, "The artist is the creation, and the performance is the celebration." This philosophy comes with its responsibilities. It means we must have, within the organization, within the staff, trainers and artists, the skills and tools to appropriately deal with the emotional, the spiritual, the physical, and the intellectual realms. It is also what makes the organization so alive, always changing, always evolving. This is where the concept of the company as a living organism and not a static organization evolved from. The staff and artists understand this. There is a great deal of respect amongst the group of people. In fact, internally, we use the word "honourable" instead of the word "professional." It is a much more powerful and relevant concept, and it resonates in the traditions of the culture—the seven teachings. This kind of thinking, this approach to creation, this reflection of the Anishinaabeg world view has recently resulted in our organization's recognition as a place of professional arts training not based on a European model. We now have the support of the National Arts Training Contribution Program of the Department of Canadian Heritage.

SH   So is it recognition in the sense of funding?

RB   Yes, operating funding to support the operations of the training facility and the student interns from across Canada, to come and share with us [The Mastin Building, Manitowaning; see Erskine, "New" 6.]. But it is also recognition of a working style, a validation of organizations that create and operate in a different way than most.

SH   So how many staff do you have now?

RB   Full-time staff—eleven. In the summer there are many more, between forty and fifty. And then there are also the student interns in the professional training program, so the company as a whole is quite large.

SH   The idea of storytelling, do you still think of this as being at the heart of what De-ba-jeh-mu-jig does?

RB   Absolutely, it's at the heart of it. But we are always looking at where storytelling meets contemporary theatre, where these things come together, and I think this show [*Ever! That Nanabush!*] is a good example.

SH   Your Board members were saying that if a script came in that the actors liked, you would do it.

RB   Absolutely. Having two distinct sources for new works—group creation through the Four Directions Creation Process, and scripted works submitted by playwrights—is a reflection of the Aboriginal arts sector in which we work. Basically, you have movement in two different directions: you have those artists who have lived, trained, been educated, and worked in the mainstream who are trying to reconnect with the cultural home community, and you have those who are from the cultural home communities who are trying to find visibility and exposure in the mainstream. The first group is much more comfortable with independently created text-based works; the second group is more in tune with non-text based group creations. Having facility in both is the goal.

SH   The facilitator, the woman you brought in from New York, Muriel Miguel, you thought would be a good person to bring in, in terms of the storytelling?

RB   Yes, the artists had heard of her and knew of other work she had done. They knew about Spiderwoman Theater, and when they read a description of her story-weaving workshop, they just thought, "Okay, well look at what we're trying to do; we've got ten stories that we're trying to weave together." They assumed that it was literally a text thing, weaving the story together, until they found out from her it was much more than that. Story-weaving was more about weaving the story through every part of your body, who you are and what you are and how you breathe, and all of those things. It turned out to be something different, but highly valuable for the process anyway. They identified her and asked if she could be brought in for a workshop.

SH   She gives workshops?

RB   Yes, lots. She is an actress, singer, director, teacher, trainer, and I am sure much more. An extraordinary woman.

SH   But last night's production [of *Ever! That Nanabush!*], those are stories that are sort of worked from script.

RB   They're worked from the stories as a resource, as a starting place, but they've applied the Four Directions creation process to them as well.

SH   Well, of course because there were some references that obviously were not in the story.

RB   All the choral work was written by Bill [Shawanda] and Sharon [King]. Well, it started out that everybody gave their feedback; each was given a story and they worked on it and presented it to the rest of the group, and then selected two people to concentrate on the stage adaptation itself and the writing of the choral work.

SH   It's amazing how they work together but they're obviously having fun. So, they get paid?

RB   Yes, everybody in the organization gets paid.

SH   Having not really lived inside the theatre world, I don't know the difference between equity and non-equity performers or if it matters.

RB   Equity performers are members of the Canadian Actor's Equity Association. This also includes directors and stage managers. For decades now, membership in Equity represented the attainment of a level of status as an artist, even though there are many professionals in the country who are not members. More recently, however, I sense this is changing, largely because the CAEA, PACT [the Professional Association of Canadian Theatres] and the Canadian Theatre Agreement that sets out the working relationship between the organizations and the artists themselves is struggling to adequately represent culturally specific organizations and artists who work in non-mainstream styles. And of course this is the fastest growing part of the sector—culturally diverse organizations. Debaj has been voicing its concerns over this struggle for a decade now, and frankly, although we have seen some significant changes at PACT, we have witnessed no changes at Equity. The frustration is building over the inability of national membership organizations to equitably represent the diversity of the communities they are mandated to serve. I think that in the not too distant future we are going to see some major shifts happening.

I think in a nutshell what has happened is that when these organizations were first established in Canada, the American model was adopted, and you know what the American model is—the melting pot, to have one set of rules that apply to everyone, to encourage everyone to be the same. Well Canada was not built on these principles. As a people and a nation we are raised to respect, accept and encourage differences—the cultural mosaic. So now that there are more and more culturally specific artists and organizations finally finding a voice and some visibility—although some have been around for 30 years or more like Black Theatre Workshop in Montreal—they are saying, "Wait a minute. We're Canadians and we don't work this way and can't work this way." So how can you be a legitimate national association and not be able to accommodate the variety of artists and working styles that exist across the country? It is working for the established mainstream organizations—they are the ones who negotiated the terms in the first place—and I understand how difficult and frightening it may seem to them that such great change is necessary. But there are really only two options: change and accommodate everyone, or establish a second set of organizations for the culturally diverse groups.

SH So there'll be another Actor's Equity, a different one? Could you belong to two?

RB Well, that's the thing—once you belong to Equity, you belong for life. There really are no provisions for leaving once you have become a member. Besides, do we really want to split the country into culturally diverse and White? Surely this is not in anyone's best interest. But the frustration is building—something has to change. Personally, I think it is a question of conflicting values. Cultural communities, certainly reserve communities, have a very different set of values than those held by mainstream society. Within the cultural community, the expectation is that each individual is an integral part of the community, with the teachings of sharing and equality. The goal is to become one with, and a part of, the community. It is circular—all things are connected—and ultimately it is a quest for respect. In the mainstream, the expectation is that you strive to rise above, to be distinguished from the rest, to be recognized for, to be a member of, etc. It is a hierarchical structure—each one for themselves, and ultimately it is a quest for status. When an artist goes from community to mainstream, these different values collide within the artist, and strain the relationship with the home community. It is a complex dynamic, and we deal with the repercussions of it on a daily basis.

SH   Are you planning a photographic history of Debaj?

RB   Well, right now we are organizing all of our visual archives and putting them on CD-roms. We are going to publish a nineteen-month English/Ojibway Calendar for our 20th Anniversary that will have photo highlights.

SH   Could you talk about custom shows? Are they whatever the community wants?

RB   Yes, a custom show is a new work commissioned by a client, like a Band Program or Health and Social Services, that explores a specific theme or issue to be presented at a conference or a gathering. The student interns research, create, and perform in these shows as part of their practicum during their training. This is one of the services of The Best Medicine Troupe, and they have created dozens of shows over the years, ranging from language retention to Metis identity, from healthy lifestyles to gambling addiction.

SH   So, before 1995 the theatre had done more of the conventional thing where you'd read the script and then you'd hire people and then everybody would disperse when it was over?

RB   Yes. It takes many years to build up enough organizational structure and resources to sustain year-round salaries. Those involved in Debaj in the early years made a lot of sacrifices—a great deal was accomplished by sweat equity and volunteerism. Not that the work itself is any easier now. Maintaining an organization of this size in the north, on an Island, and always susceptible to the whims of government funding policy, we still make a great deal of sacrifices, especially in terms of our personal lives.

But we made a significant change in the organization in 1995. Everything was up in the air. There were so many cuts to arts funding with the new provincial government, and theatre organizations closing left, right, and centre. It was a scary time. We also began to reassess the pattern of spending years training local artists and then losing them to the city. We needed to be able to keep our artists in the north, but ensure that they enjoyed the opportunities that other artists in the country had access to. It meant defining a second role for our artists, a second skill set that could sustain their employment. That is when we began to invest in training our artists to be trainers themselves. This decision was the impetus for developing the entire outreach program of our company and, subsequently, the professional training. In 1995 we literally turned our chairs around and stopped measuring ourselves against what was happening in southern Ontario, in Toronto. We began to see ourselves in reference to the rest of the province, the north, the isolated and remote communities, the cultural home communities, the reserves and settlements across the country. This was a very empowering experience for our company. Suddenly, we understood who we were, and how we fit with the national theatre scene.

SH   And whose idea was that, to turn the chairs around?

RB   I think it just happened out of frustration. We thought it was an act of defiance; it turned out to be an act of self-discovery.

SH   Was it mainly for financial reasons that you did that? As you said there were no resources; they had kind of run dry. There was no other artistic director appearing.

RB   See, what happened was that we posted for an artistic director at this same time. Well, in this sector there just aren't a lot of experienced human resources to draw on. Native theatre is still in its infancy in this country. So we decided to invest in the development of the artists who had already demonstrated a commitment to the company, knowing that this would take several years of development. For the most part, the terms we use to describe our roles in the organization are for the benefit of the outside world. Within the organization, we may have a different and much more complex understanding of how we make decisions, how we articulate our vision, etc. We announced that Audrey Debassige would become the Associate Artistic Director, I would become the Artistic Producer, and Joe Osawabine, Chris Wemigwans, Bill Shawanda, and Bruce Naokwegijig would become company Animators. Artistic decisions have been made by this association of artists. We determined that we were committed to the development of local artists, and this meant giving them a voice and participation in all artistic decisions. This investment in their futures and their development was a conscious decision, and it has paid off in spades. Some of the animators are more interested in the development of new works and the professional creation activities of the company, while others have a greater interest in the training and outreach, allowing us to continue to serve our clients in the north where we had been touring regularly...

SH   Northern Ontario?

RB   Northern Ontario particularly.

SH But you're doing a lot in Saskatchewan, I noticed. *The Dreaming Beauty* is touring.

RB *The Dreaming Beauty* is touring Saskatchewan.

SH But that's sort of different. That's not necessarily outreach.

RB That is a dissemination activity, with an outreach component to bridge to the Native communities. We showcased our work at Saskatchewan Contact in Kindersley and subsequently were booked to conduct a tour through OSAC.

SH What is OSAC?

RB The Organization of Saskatchewan Arts Councils.

SH And why Saskatchewan? Just because they have another good Native theatre in Saskatoon [Saskatchewan Native Theatre Company]?

RB Not really. More because of the vision of Nancy Martin who works at OSAC, and who said for several years, "we have to get you guys out here. We have such a large Native population in our province." Actually, Saskatchewan Native Theatre Company did not even exist when Nancy first inquired about our company. Nancy kept seeing us at different contacts and showcase events, and said, "I don't know how I'm going to do it but I'm going to have to get you into the province of Saskatchewan." And so many things happen that way in our sector—we call it the curriculum of opportunity. We still are not integrated into the mainstream networks. It is usually the initiative of a single individual who meets our company, sees our work, and says, "we need you; let's find a way to do it." But I must say that as an organization we've put a lot of work into facilitating how that might happen. What we are actually doing is constantly trying to bridge between Native and non-Native communities.

There is no cross-cultural infrastructure in our country. Our artists know how to bridge. They have had anti-racism training, cross-cultural facilitation training, Neuro-Linguistic Programming Training, the list goes on. And every student in our professional training program receives the same training.

SH What else are you involved in right now?

RB We've been invited to be Artists in Residence at the Art Gallery of Ontario in February and March of 2003. Looks like a very exciting project—"Audge's Place: All Things are Connected." We will be creating an installation that is a replica of Audrey's actual kitchen and living room here in Wiky. Her home has been a meeting place, a place of convergence for visiting and local artists, for many years. We will recreate it in the Zack's Gallery, with actors physically present on the set. Gallery visitors will be encouraged to enter the house, take off their shoes, and interact with the performers as if they are visiting the reserve itself. They can have some Indian corn soup, pick up an instrument and play music, ask questions about the family photos on the wall or the sticky notes on the fridge, all of which will be authentic. The idea is to confront stereotypes about Native people by providing a one-on-one opportunity to meet, to share, to eat, to begin to build a relationship. Our artists will answer any questions asked about their culture, their lives, their experience, but always from the perspective of being in Wiky. We will also be inviting other Aboriginal artists from southern Ontario to drop in whenever they can, just as it happens at home. And there are many other parts to this project; we will have artists delivering workshops with both elementary and secondary schools in collaboration with other urban based artists. We will have artists in residence at the partnering institutions including the Gardiner Museum and Harbourfront Centre. We are also presenting scenes from *Ever! That Nanabush!* in Walker Court during March Break. It is a very loaded month with a great deal of networking and collaboration opportunities, not to mention the visibility for our company in Toronto. We are extremely excited about the project.

SH So, it's an exhibit at the AGO [Art Gallery of Ontario] in Toronto, and your people are physically present as well?

RB Yes, a living exhibit with improvisation around the fact that they will only respond as if they are really in Wikwemikong and not in Toronto. The phone will ring; people will always be coming and going, hanging out. We want to create the feeling of community that we experience at home, as much as possible.

SH What do they call those? I've never heard of those at the AGO.

RB They call them artists in residence and usually they're for a single person. This is the first time a theatre company has been invited to be artist in residence. It is through the education department at the AGO, and it is part of the celebration of the new installations of contemporary and historical Aboriginal visual culture in the Canadian Wing. An important part of our involvement is to assist the staff and docents of the AGO in developing a richer understanding of the Anishinaabeg world view so they are better equipped to share information about the collections in the future. We will be delivering additional workshops to these people, as well as sitting on a public panel to discuss the outcomes of the project, and networking, networking and more networking.

SH   So that will be next year?

RB   That will be the last two weeks of February and the first two weeks of March [2003]. Some of the AGO staff are coming up next weekend to meet with us again, and see the show.

SH   That will be fun. Well, I should let you go; I feel like I've kept you here all day.

Joe Osawabine

[W]hen people come to another country it's the same Mother, it's the same land, but there is something that's a bit different. I know what that is, but I don't really know how to explain it. So, somehow, people have to be able to bring that memory with them, or try to nurture it, or midwife it, so that it's here.

And I believe that can happen. My great-grandfather was from Scotland, and his mother was Irish, and in the last few years I've heard their voices. There is this circle that says, "Well we are your Grandmothers, too, we are your Grandfathers, too." And I have never been to those countries.

So, I believe that the people who come to Canada, or who have been in Canada for generations, who say "this is our land" and "this is our culture" and "this is where it is," if they are really artists and writers, how can they not hear those voices? How can they not hear them?

—Maria Campbell, *Contemporary Challenges*, 63

That this particular mythology [North American Aboriginal] is every bit as colourful, as magical, as distinct, and as powerful as any mythology the whole world over... should require small explanation. What may [require explanation] is that, when held up to other world mythologies, whether Greek, Celtic, Egyptian, Christian, Hindu, Buddhist or otherwise, it ranks right up there among the oldest, the most improbably ancient, together, that is, with other Aboriginal mythologies from Australia, Japan's island of Hokkaido, and circumpolar regions such as Siberia, Greenland, and Scandinavia. 40,000, 50,000, even 60,000 years have been cited, by one school of archaeology or another, by one visionary or another, as possible life spans for such ancient bodies of "narrative," of oral literature. So the extent to which North American Aboriginal mythology could be said, in effect, to be the psychological, emotional, and spiritual "map" of ancient North America, right down to the birth of its human history, would not be that much of an exaggeration.

—Tomson Highway, *A Trickster Tale* playbill,
"Who is the Trickster?" 2

— • – • —

My interview with the current Artistic Director of De-ba-jeh-mu-jig, Joe Osawabine, took place at a barbecue at Wikwemikong, cooked by Joe Osawabine and me, on 10 August 2003, after the barbecue and before Joe's performance in the lead role of A Trickster Tale *that evening.*

— • – • —

SH We were just talking about the project that De-ba-jeh-mu-jig is doing with the theatre in Prague. What's the project called?

JO What I've been calling it is "Myths that Unite Us" so it's a universal mythology theme: what are some of the similarities within mythology that everybody has? It's a project between De-ba-jeh-mu-jig, the University of Toronto, and the Prague theatre company [Studio Ypsilon]. We all work with the same themes and the same information. They develop over there a piece based on the themes and information they have and at the same time we're developing over here based on the same information. Then we come together and we put the two shows together to create one show. We'll tour it to Toronto, Manitoulin Island, and Montreal. They'll fly over here and they'll bring another performance piece with them as well that they want to kind of showcase over here. Then we fly over there and we stay there for a week performing. We take a show with us and so we're going to take *A Trickster Tale* which is what we're doing right now.

SH Is it an Aboriginal company in Prague, or mainstream European?

JO It's a European company.

SH You've been involved in this theatre since you were twelve and you're twenty-four now.

JO Half of my life! [Laughter.]

SH And you're about to become the Artistic Director.

JO As of next season, starting in April. After this project [the current run of *A Trickster Tale*], I'm starting to look into places where I can go and do apprenticeships with other theatre companies in Canada. We're thinking of maybe Firehall Theatre in B.C., creation companies that work similarly to De-ba-jeh-mu-jig and are relatively the same size.

SH Creation companies?

JO Meaning that we create all the work that we produce rather than bring in scripts and just do totally scripted pieces all the time, which we also do. Like Tomson Highway has this one but generally we're a creation company, like *New World Brave* used the creation process, and last year's *Ever! That Nanabush!* also used the Four Directions creation process.

SH So you'll continue with the Four Directions process.

JO That's something that I've been thinking about and it's starting to gain momentum. We're still figuring out what exactly it is. We have a good understanding of how it works but it's still evolving. Working with the kids in James Bay, when we did go up north in January, we used the Four Directions creation process as a way to help them create.

We integrated them right into the show by the end of the week. And then from there that's how we picked the eight most promising and brought them down here for a six-week theatre intensive and then we send them back home and hopefully they do something while they're in their own communities. So from the eight of them we're going to pick two more who might want to stay on for the year-long internship.

SH Internships involve them in the mainstage production?

JO We're reworking that. It's been in the past that they were part of the mainstage crew. I think what our idea is now is to have them go through all the steps ending in the mainstage production, right? So they go through the whole year and if the show's appropriate at the time then they end their internship that way.

SH They're involved in all the aspects of the theatre?

JO Pretty much. When these custom shows come up, like when there's a conference on diabetes or whatever, they're involved in the whole creation of the show and also just like the day-to-day activities that need to be taken care of. It depends on the internship. We have a few who are on the production internship so they focus mainly on the production end of things where if they're here on a performance internship then they focus more on the creation of the shows.

SH Are you using the new site, the Mastin Building in Manitowaning?

JO Ya! That came at the right time. We've been using it so much.

SH   Do you think ultimately you'll have performances there?

JO   That's the plan. We're planning to turn it into a 100-seat black box theatre so that we can have our own performances there during the winter and also other companies can rent the space. We're talking about maybe utilizing our interns for that. Say somebody has a script they want to develop; they bring maybe a director or a dramaturge and they bring the script but they utilize our actors to workshop it.

SH   De-ba-jeh-mu-jig has really grown over the twenty years with all the new programs. Do you think it will continue to grow? How might it?

JO   It's growing continually faster than we can keep up with it. This project [Prague] is our first international project where we're actually flying overseas. That's a first for De-ba-jeh-mu-jig. We've been all across Canada and into the States but never overseas.

SH   You're growing in terms of geography…

JO   We're growing in terms of geography but also the profile of the company and the quality of the work is continually getting better. The profile is gaining some weight out there. We talk about De-ba-jeh-mu-jig not as an organization but more as an organism which gives it life, right? Rather than working for the company, the people who work in the company *are* the company. It's the people who make up De-ba-jeh-mu-jig, not so much the buildings. If that's all De-ba-jeh-mu-jig is, then it's just a run-down old trailer on the middle of an island in northern Ontario. [Laughter.] But the people make it what it is. It's growing and living the way the people do. The more the people evolve and grow creatively and personally and artistically, the more the company develops.

SH   Do you think the place of storytelling in Native theatre and culture is important?

JO   I think it's very important. That's the whole reason why we're here, to share our stories. Traditional storytelling has—I don't want to say died—but it's not as present anymore. So this is just a contemporary version of the tradition. We're still telling stories as a theatre company because of the themes that De-ba-jeh-mu-jig chooses to work with, the revitalization of the Anishinaabeg culture. It's to keep the stories alive in an interesting way that the younger people will take interest in, so that they want to get involved with the company or find their own way to share their stories. We tell our own personal stories as well as stories from the culture. Like last year was *Ever! That Nanabush!* and that's a traditional character, the Trickster character, and it's bringing those back. I remember reading those books in school. My mother remembers reading those books in school, which is the Daphne Odjig series. So everybody in the community has read these books and then they kind of just sat on the shelves. They stopped using them in the school curriculum so now we're bringing them back to life in a new way.

SH Maybe it helps reinforce a sense of identity. *A Trickster Tale* is in some ways a traditional story, too.

JO It's a traditional character. The story has the traditional elements from the stories that were told, like about the Trickster tricking the rabbits into dancing with their eyes closed so that he can kill them while they're dancing. He figures out how to manipulate these rabbits. But it's more a contemporary version. This particular show is more about entertainment value than the actual morals of the story, and the way I see it is that this show is there so that people can laugh, for the healing power of laughter and its traditional role in Native culture. A lot of Native people will laugh in time of crisis or make jokes if the situation is really bad. This is about bringing back the laughter.

SH What would you like said about De-ba-jeh-mu-jig in this history? Is it what it's done for young people?

JO Ya, I think that's where I'd put my focus—the importance of telling stories and having a way for these younger kids to see themselves reflected on the stage. In European theatre or classical theatre—they don't relate to Shakespeare; they don't relate to Chekhov. These big spectacular shows like *The Lion King*, sure they're entertaining, but there's nothing that speaks to them about who they are, so I think that's the importance of De-ba-jeh-mu-jig. We are a place where these young people can see themselves reflected in their own stories.

SH Is the emphasis on the young also traditional? If you take care of the next generation, then...

JO Ya, if you take care of the younger generation then you're ensured that there is a future.

SH We were talking about another theatre that advertised *A Trickster Tale* as a children's story.

JO It could be in the sense that all the characters are all very animated and entertaining in that way. They're so much larger than life that the children could be drawn into the world but there is a lot of sexual innuendo. It's about consumption and food, but knowing Tomson you know what he's getting at. [Laughter.] A lot of families have been coming out to the show and maybe that stuff does go right over the kids' head and it really is about the Trickster being hungry and trying to get food, literally. The kids really enjoy the show because the characters are so animated and big. It's so fast-paced that it's more up to the speed the kids are used to. Life has gotten so fast that they need it fast. Like TV is so many frames per second and it needs to be that fast.

This is something that we've been talking about actually for a little while, the pacing of Native theatre and the stories. The pace is so slow sometimes for a non-Native audience, but for the older Native people that's the pace that they move in, right? So it's trying to find the balance. This one is that high-energy show and it's over before you know it.

SH   Is changing the pacing part of making it contemporary?

JO   That could be a good way of doing that. It's contemporary in the sense of the costumes and the music that the characters are singing. There's one point where we're practically having a hoedown, and there's no traditional music in the show. One of the grandsons is dressed in a rave outfit like he's ready to head out to the dance club.

SH   What most interests you about Native theatre in general? Do you see other Native plays?

JO   Yes, but it's kind of hard living up here on Manitoulin. There's not really a place to go to see even other theatre in general let alone Native theatre, right? We are one of the main Native theatre companies in Canada and so it's like we are the place where you'd go to see Native theatre. [Laughter.] There's Saskatchewan Native Theatre Company, Native Earth in Toronto.... Just that we have to go through this much conversation to try and figure out the Native theatre companies in Canada says a little something about it in itself.

SH   During the run of "Audge's Place" at the AGO last spring you saw a play in Toronto…

JO   *Time Stands Still* [by Terry Ivins, at Theatre Passe Muraille in association with Native Earth Performing Arts]. It was good, a two-person show. One thing about Native theatre is that for the older generation, people who are more around my mom's age, for them it was a healing process. It was a way to tell their stories about the residential schools and all the hardships that came out of that; it was a way to break the silence and speak about the abuse, the alcoholism that they grew up with, and that's not to say that those problems no longer exist or that all the work that came from that generation was a personal healing process, but art reflects life and life reflects art. So that's what you end up seeing a lot of. I think that being from the next generation down, other than the fact that many of us don't speak the language, we aren't directly affected by the residential school system, or all the hardships that the generation above me went through. The effects of residential schools have been filtered down somewhat so we're coming at it with new concerns. Like *New World Brave*, for instance. It explores what the young Native male's role in society is. Traditionally we would've been hunters, gatherers, trappers, providers for the family and caregivers, so what is our role today now that we're not hunting? We're coming at it with new stories and as a form of self expression, not as a way of dealing with our past. We acknowledge our past but look to the future. Native theatre now is more about hope for the future than it is about the hardships of the past.

SH Is the theatre a source of employment for the young, too?

JO It is and it isn't. De-ba-jeh-mu-jig is doing really well right now. We have thirty-two people that are on the payroll. They're interns and summer students and full-time staff and the director and the production designer, positions like that. But then when the summer's over we'll go down to eight for the rest of the year. My friend Greg [Odjig] and his brother are here and they're both actors. Greg is alumni with De-ba-jeh-mu-jig and so is Jonathan [Fisher]. They started out here, but then they went to Toronto because the work was so scarce here at the time. We were really struggling, just living contract to contract. We'd go for two weeks and then we'd be unemployed for maybe a month and then we'd have another gig, a conference, so we'd be employed for two weeks again. But now we're beyond that. It's finally paying off, all the volunteering that we did in our earlier years. [Laughter.]

But Greg moved off to Toronto; Jonathan moved off to Toronto to find that work. They joined Equity and being Native—I hate to say it—but you get typecast as a Native person. How many plays out there call for a Native person? So it's trying to find other roads. Now if Greg wants to come back to De-ba-jeh-mu-jig because now we do have places for him, it would be so hard for us to employ him because he's Equity and De-ba-jeh-mu-jig is a non-Equity company. The older generations all joined Equity, like Pukaney. We worked with Jeffrey Eshkawkogan [Pukaney] a few years back. He did one play that was an Equity show and all of a sudden he became an Equity member without even knowing it. So now years later we hired him for a role and Equity said he owed eight years of dues, and now we have to pay his dues so that we could employ one of the artists from our own community and go through all the Equity rules and regulations to do so because now Pukaney is an Equity member. And all because of one show he did eight years prior? Equity doesn't make sense for us. It's a different lifestyle up here in the north and it just doesn't make sense for us to apply all the Equity rules and regulations, although we do pay our artists Equity rates! [Laughter.]

SH   Theatre helps young people with self-esteem.

JO   I started at a fairly young age when I was twelve. When you're thirteen, fourteen that's when you start becoming aware of how you are in your body and you just feel totally awkward and you think people are always judging you based on how you look. I started before I even got to that point so I was out there and I didn't really care the way I looked on stage or whatever and then when I did get to that point I was comfortable enough and I had enough confidence that I just sailed through it. That's one of the important things about theatre, the sense of self that it gives to these young kids, which is what we're doing with the kids from James Bay, right? They're so underserved up there in the north. That's one of De-ba-jeh-mu-jig's commitments is to go to these underserved Native communities in the North and bring it to them. Hopefully they take some ownership after, and it's theirs, right? Our hope is that these young people are gonna go up there and start their own theatre troupes or performing groups and start doing conferences, which is what happened with the group we worked with in Grassy Narrows back in about '96. We did three years with them and then they kind of just took off and they're doing conferences and developing all their own pieces and stuff like that.

SH   Do you mean they're doing custom shows for conferences, like for the CNIB or the Diabetes Society?

JO   They create their own shows for different conferences.

SH   Do you work with computers a lot?

JO   We have another project underway right now, an Internet project through the University of Waterloo. We're going to have an Internet console here—this is all indigenous peoples—and there's going to be another company in Australia that's gonna have another Internet console that connects directly with ours and then another one in Africa, and we're all linked that way. So then we create, we improvise, we collaborate through the Internet on these three continents. Anybody can log on at any time and see what's going on. On August 22nd the professor who's doing it, Gerhard Hauck, has a conference where he's showing his delegates his project, the unveiling kind of thing, and so at the conference we're going to be here on the island and at the conference through the Internet.

SH   So it's a visual connection, too?

JO   Ya, it's visual and audio. There's about a half a second delay and he's trying to work on that.

SH   Let your imagination run wild. If you could do anything as Artistic Director next year, what would you do? [Laughter.] If you had unlimited resources… [More laughter.]

JO   If I had unlimited resources [Laughter.], proper facilities, new equipment, a touring bus… [Lots of laughter.] Actually one of the themes I've been thinking about for the upcoming season is "Connecting our elders with our youth as a way of connecting our past with our future." I haven't really thought about any specific projects yet but that theme seems important to me. It's like we said before: take care of the younger generation and we are ensuring a future. It's the elders who carry the stories of the past. We need to pass these stories on to the younger generations, people like myself and younger if these stories are going to live on. If we don't do something about preserving these stories right now then traditional storytelling will die as the elders pass on. We have to keep these stories alive even if it is in a contemporary style such as theatre. We need to give hope for the future generations by sharing with the younger generations now the wisdom of generations past. Let them stand up and be proud of who they are and where they come from.

Also embedded in that same theme of connecting our past with our future are the issues around the language. The elders are also the ones who carry the language with them. There aren't too many young people who can speak fluently, at least not here in Wiky, so by connecting the elders with the youth we would also be giving opportunity for the young people to be in an environment where the language is spoken fluently. I think the theatre offers an excellent opportunity for these two generations who seem worlds apart to connect with each other again. Our elders are our teachers.…

Another project that's been lingering in my head since Ron [Berti] and I talked about it is that the people in the community here, Wikwemikong, don't have an understanding of the history of the community. Like I don't, anyway, and anybody I really talk to doesn't either. We know a lot of the main things that happened like when we never signed the land away—we're unceded—and that gives the people here a sense of pride. So one of the projects I've been thinking about is the history of Wikwemikong. I know *The Manitoulin Incident* was sort of that but it was more about Manitoulin in general. I want this one to be more specifically about Wikwemikong. This is for the community. I don't think it would make much sense to take it outside. But who knows, eh? I want to do maybe a hundred-year span about the evolution of the community. So it could start off all in Ojibway and who was the Chief at the time. We can get a hold of some of the Chiefs' speeches through the Band Office and records and bring it right into the present. And as the language evolved in the community so it would evolve in the play so that by the end of the play it's mostly in English and broken Ojibway, and it's hard for the young people to be speaking the language and communicating with Elders because a lot of the Elders only speak in the language. They can't communicate with their grandchildren. That's another project I've been thinking about.

I would also like shows such as *A Trickster Tale*, contemporary shows that deal with Native culture. We've got to find some way to break through the mainstream market so that we're out there and we're representing people in a positive light on the world stage.

Reprise: Interview with
Joe Osawabine and Ron Berti

27 December 2005. Wikwemikong, Ontario. Audrey Wemigwans's kitchen.

— · – · —

SH   We haven't talked about De-ba-jeh-mu-jig's more recent productions, *The Gift* and *The Promise*, for example.

JO   Two years ago [2003] I was just starting to talk about the idea of connecting our elders with our youth as a way of connecting our past with our future. Since then we've taken some steps along that path working with cultural elder and spiritual advisor, Eddie King. A very new way of creating works is by going back to the foundation teachings. The foundation teachings are specific teachings that were actually carved in stone [petroglyphs] to be passed on to us as a way of life. We referenced the petroglyphs that are located in Peterborough because those are the ones that Eddie uses, the ones he was taught with and the ones that are most accessible to us. There are petroglyphs across North America or Turtle Island but we used those specific petroglyphs. For the production of *The Gift*, we looked at the foundation teachings very literally, and explored how these very old teachings can still be relevant in today's society. The foundation teachings include Time, Freedom, Life, The Four Axes, Ceremony, and the Preservation of Humanity, and again there are a number of teachings that go with each. We also looked at the idea of contemporary storytelling versus traditional storytelling and theatre as a form of contemporary storytelling. So am I a theatre artist performing in a play? Or am I a descendent of our ancestors partaking in traditional storytelling? What is our role as a theatre company to our traditional stories? And if we aren't telling our stories then who will? Like I said, it all begins with the foundation teachings so that we can remain true to the foundation teachings and what they were there for in the first place, which is to teach us how to live a better way of life, a way of life that we as a people seem to have strayed off from. Our ancestors have literally carved these in stone teachings for us to live our everyday lives by, so it's about going back to those ideas and looking at them first and making sure that everything in the production is centred and grounded in those teachings. The idea of freedom—we all have the freedom to create, and we all have the freedom not to create as well, so it really leaves a choice for us to decide if we want to do this or not, and we decided that we do.

The Indian Affairs, which was our last mainstage production, in 2005, also started from the same place, the foundation teachings, but looking more at the idea of relationships and family, specifically male-female relationships and the way we interact in these intimate relationships with each other; and, what is family? One of the main teachings that *The Indian Affairs* was centred around was the legend of the first dream, regarding a woman who did not know how to take care of her child: she was then given in a dream, a simple one-line statement which was, "watch the wolves." The idea behind that lesson or that teaching of "watch the wolves" is that wolves will display all of the seven teachings in everything that they do within their packs and all their concern is for the preservation of the pack. The males would actually—we learned this from Eddie—the males will actually give food out of their mouths to the females of the pack if the food is that scarce, and all the females are taken care of first. So you can apply those teachings over to our everyday life, making sure that by taking care of the females we ensure the preservation of the pack, or humanity in this case, which again relates directly back to the foundation teachings. We also wanted to express this idea that the teachings are always present—you've seen the show—the idea behind Evelyn Roy and Doreen Peltier's characters, the "Spirit Wolves," that they were constantly present throughout the show up on the rock there and sometimes, well most times, totally unnoticed by the other characters in the show... but they were there and the teachings are there constantly. You have to seek them out, these teachings, because it's not that the teachings aren't there or that they died or something. They are there, they're present, but you have to seek them out for yourself... and when you take the time to seek them out for yourself then that's when they'll present themselves to you, right?

SH   Can you talk a bit about *The Promise*?

JO   *The Promise* was De-ba-jeh-mu-jig's first full-scale dance production. It was directed and choreographed by Karen Pheasant.

RB   It is important to the director and choreographer, Karen Pheasant, that artists learn the original meaning and intent of the dances, and understand that it is their responsibility to do this. *The Promise* is based on an actual event, a personal experience of Karen's, and her journey and her learning is interpreted through this dance piece.

JO It was the jingle dress dance, a healing dance. She attended a Pow wow where the elders who knew the original dance were at the Pow wow and stood in the circle and taught the younger generation the original steps of the dance. Because what happens is that, I guess just like everything, the dance evolved and the steps became contemporary steps—a lot of fancy footwork and things like that—where the original dance was just plain and simple, which also ties in nicely to an idea that we were exploring with *The Gift*, the idea that these things need to be plain and simple and orderly and sincere, but I think most of all… sincere. So both shows that summer were about going back to the roots or at least looking at the original ideas and intentions behind storytelling, and what the original intention behind a particular dance was—a common theme that year.

RB There was a very interesting quality of authenticity to the production of *The Promise*. At the original gathering upon which it is based, dancers danced for a group of grandmothers, then watched the grandmothers dance, then danced again themselves, back and forth until the dance was transferred accurately. This element was not just represented, but built into the work, as each night a selection of grandmothers from the community appeared on stage to watch the young dancers.

SH Could you say something about *Your Dream Was Mine* from 2004, by Shirley Cheechoo and Greta Cheechoo?

JO It was like coming full circle. Shirley Cheechoo wrote this play and, you know, I don't know if she ever considered that De-ba-jeh-mu-jig would be the ones to produce it. She is the founder of the company and so it was important for us when the opportunity arose to have produced this play. We're still in full support of the artists who paved the way for us to begin the kind of works that we are producing today, and vice versa— Shirley is still supporting the company after all these years. Hmmm what else? Oh yah! It was also a full Equity production so it gave us an opportunity to engage some of the artists from our community that are Equity, an opportunity that doesn't come up very often.

SH So we can move to the other two from 2005, *How Will You Remember Me?*, first of all.

JO *How Will You Remember Me?* was a specific request for Aboriginal Solidarity Day at the Museum of Civilization [Gatineau, Quebec] and the overall theme this year was V-Day, the sixtieth-year anniversary, honouring our veterans and our elders, and so that was a specific request for us to produce a play that deals with honouring Aboriginal veterans who served in world wars. We actually went out and talked to people who served in the wars and got the stories from our veterans in our community and translated some of the stories onto the stage, not any specific story but just the overall general feelings people had and why they chose to go serve in the first place, and we portrayed that on stage. It was a very good turnout at all performances. After the Quebec shows we performed the play for audiences here in Wiky on Canada Day.

SH And then your first French-language production.

JO *Shtaa-taa-haa! Nanabush!* was an adaptation of a production we did in 2002, *Ever! That Nanabush!*. We were approached by Jean-Guy Girard, the Artistic Director of Flash Fête, a festival which took place in Alma, Quebec. The festival is thirty-six hours of non-stop performance which sounded like a cool festival that we wanted to be a part of, and at the time when he approached us to do it we were gonna take *A Trickster Tale* because that's the show that we had up and running at the time, but for whatever reason it didn't happen that year [2003] and so we did it this year. We were trying to decide what show to do and still contemplating *A Trickster Tale* but not having the full cast here we thought, "what would be the best way to approach this?" And *Ever! That Nanabush!* we thought would be fun to do because you can use a lot of imagery and movement, and then it developed one step further. I think it just happened that Geneviève Pineault of TN-O [Théâtre du Nouvel-Ontario, Sudbury's professional French-language theatre] emailed us and just wanted to let us know that she's there [as Artistic Director] and that we should find ways to collaborate because our companies have similar qualities and interests. This came up and we thought, "let's call Geneviève to come and help us work on *Shtaa-taa-haa! Nanabush!* and actually do a French version of the Nanabush show," because the festival was taking place in Quebec and the audience was ninety-nine per cent French speaking. So working with her, we took the Nanabush stories and didn't translate the text but reworked the stories in French. So it wasn't just a literal translation of an existing show; it was a new show, incorporating French key words so that the audience could follow the storyline through. It was funny and quite a challenge because we... first of all we don't speak French. [Laughter.] Jean-Guy emailed us later to tell us how surprised he was that the show was "*en* *français*" so that was cool. You know, it doesn't take a whole lot of effort to take that one extra step and meet people where they are, and people generally appreciate it.

SH　Could you talk about the National Aboriginal Arts Animator Program?

RB　We now have formally put in place and announced the National Aboriginal Arts Animator Program which is a three-year program of professional training for Aboriginal, Métis and Inuit artists from across Canada. The goal of the program is to train and support the development of Arts Animators, who are professional artists with a dual focus of personal expertise in a field, *and* skills and resources for community engagement through the arts.

Our programs are unique and are culturally and socially specific, utilizing for example, the 4D Creation Process for developing new works, validating the traditions of orality, integrating foundation teachings, observational and operational learning, etc. We are responding to the infrastructure development needs of the Aboriginal arts sector as a whole, by training multi-skilled professional artists in association with community cultural and economic development.

The actual practicum the students are engaged in is always in association with professional artists. It includes the design and delivery of training residencies and workshops in communities including urban, rural, and isolated and remote, the developing and producing of custom shows, collaborations with other artists and organizations, showcasing, networking, touring, etc. A successful arts animator is an artist who is skilled at identifying and utilizing available resources—physical, human, financial, material, environmental, etc.—and who is adept at working across sectors.

SH　One of your current brochures emphasizes bridge building. Can you say more about that?

RB　De-ba-jeh-mu-jig over time has realized that it plays a unique role as a bridge: between north and south, between youth and elder, between Native and non-Native, between traditional and contemporary. This unique positioning has taught us many things about working cross-culturally, about respecting world views, about both community values and mainstream values, about sharing and respect. We believe that what we have learned is of value to many other Canadians, and we are organizing to be able to offer programs and services to share these learnings.

SH   Do you see an influence of De-ba-jeh-mu-jig's method on mainstream theatre?

RB   Yes I do see an influence, and in many places. We have certainly influenced cultural policy and program design in organizations from arts funders to national theatre associations. We have influenced organizations like Soulpepper Theatre Company who have acknowledged that their professional training model is an adaptation of ours. And we have influenced organizations from Harbourfront Centre to the Art Gallery of Ontario through our outreach and education programs which promote alternative ways of working that reflect alternative world views. But perhaps most important is the influence that will continue to occur over time, between our artists and individual artists from the mainstream, and from the relationships built upon engaging in partnership and co-creation.

Conclusion

> [T]here's something happening in Native American writing, and it has to do with the old stories. There are a number of us who are going back to the old stories and using them, or they are using us, as a means of telling a contemporary story....
>
> It seems to me that maybe at this time in the history of the world we need to go back to those. Because I see a big change coming in the world itself, and in the way that human beings relate to the Earth, to our existence here.... What I see past the rocky time is something incredibly exciting.... I see a new beginning, the fifth generation coming into being, or the "Fifth World" as the Hopis call it.... I also see that down the road, someday, we are going to come to terms with cultural differences, with racism, and it is going to free up humanity to do better things than to kill each other.
>
> —Beth Cuthand, in *Contemporary Challenges: Conversations with Canadian Native Authors*, 40.

— • – • —

De-ba-jeh-mu-jig Theatre, with its focus on the creation and presentation of Aboriginal stories, has had an unaccountable impact on Native theatre in Canada and beyond in its twenty-three years, and it seems only a matter of time before its impact will be more fully felt in non-Native theatre as well. Historically, the Native Canadian eye has always witnessed the life of this land; now we will begin to hear, more and more, through the work of De-ba-jeh-mu-jig and other theatres like it, what that eye saw, how it perceived European contact and other large and small events told almost exclusively in the past from the point of view of the immigrants and passers by. A few cases of documentation will serve to show that a Native perspective has always been gestured towards by mainstream writers. We have always known that the perspective exists but we have only begun to explore its wisdom and truths.

In an article published in 1930 in the *Canadian Historical Review*, Margaret M. Cameron traces the ill-fated beginnings of theatre in New France in the seventeenth century, reminding us throughout the article that the original inhabitants of what is now Quebec were characters and actors in the first French plays on this soil, as well as spectators of them. Cameron writes that "a few Indian words" (9) appeared in what we usually refer to as the first Canadian play, Marc Lescarbot's piece of 1606 called *Théâtre de Neptune en la Nouvelle France représenté sur les flots de Port Royal le quatorzième de novembre mille six cent au retour du sieur de Poutrincourt du païs de Armouchiquios*; indeed, one of the justifications for theatre in New France—theatre being condemned by the Catholic hierarchy for its demonic effect on morals—was its role in converting Natives (10). Plays were usually produced in this colony to celebrate the coming of a new Quebec governor and typically included what Cameron describes as three groups of characters: "the Frenchmen, who speak in verse; the converted Indians and the allegorical figures such as the genius of the forests, who speak in French prose; and the unconverted savages who speak in their own tongues" (12). In *Performing Canada: The Nation Enacted in the Imagined Theatre*, Alan Filewod also discusses Lescarbot's *The Theatre of Neptune in New France* but claims that the Aboriginal characters in the first French-Canadian play in fact spoke in verse:

> Neptune's aboriginal supplicants were probably portrayed by Frenchmen, but, as Lescarbot tells us, they were watched by the settlement's aboriginal neighbours. What did they make of this moment, as they saw their identities re-enacted by the colonizers? And what did they understand of the perfectly phrased couplets with which the enacted "Savages" deployed classical allusion to offer their world to the King of France...? We don't know because of course, nobody asked them.... Two sets of eyes saw two very different events. (iii–xiv)

With De-ba-jeh-mu-jig's rediscovery of these stories from the Native point of view, Canadian history becomes reshaped and so our memories and imaginations transformed.

The results of telling great tales of the past from the Aboriginal point of view have not always been welcome. Erika Behrisch records the effects of Dr. John Rae's report, submitted in 1854, on the failed Franklin Expedition to the Canadian Arctic. The English Sir John Franklin and his crews had set out in 1845 to discover the Northwest Passage and none of them survived. Rae's report to the British Admiralty, which was based on the testimony of Inuit reporters who had heard the stories told and retold, concluded that the Franklin crews had resorted to cannibalism in their last days. Disseminated by the British Admiralty, these stories created tremendous retaliation in the press because, to quote Ian Stone, "Royal naval personnel did not eat each other and that was that" (qtd. in Behrisch, 58). Doubt was cast upon the truth of Rae's report explicitly because it relied on tales told by Natives.

But those very tales we are now coming to see as providing necessary truths about life on this land, truths without which we will never be able to know the past, present, or future accurately. Stories teach us how to know those truths. De-ba-jeh-mu-jig Theatre in its twenty-three years in northern Ontario has started the process of learning the tales, telling them again and again, and showing others how. As such it holds a unique and essential place in Canadian theatre history and in the Canadian identity itself. For in traditional storytelling, the tales of our own lives become inextricably linked with the tales of our place, family, beliefs, dreams, historical and cultural milieus. As such our lives become somehow more meaningful and less singular at the same time.

Appendix

Materials included in this Appendix have been composed and provided by De-ba-jeh-mu-jig Theatre.

Production Chronology 1981 – 2006

Respect the Voice of the Child, by Shirley Cheechoo and Billy Merasty
Shadow People, by Shirley Cheechoo
A Ridiculous Spectacle in One Act, by Tomson Highway
Ayash, by Jim Morris
Nothing Personal, by Shirley Cheechoo and Alanis King
Aria, by Tomson Highway
Nanabush of the 80s, by Kennetch Charlette, Shirley Cheechoo,
    and Alanis King
The Rez Sisters, by Tomson Highway
Toronto at Dreamer's Rock, by Drew Hayden Taylor
Education is Our Right, by Drew Hayden Taylor
The Thunderbird Children, by Esther Jacko
Word Magic, by Lenore Keeshig-Tobias
Pictures on the Wall, by Drew Hayden Taylor
The Bootlegger Blues, by Drew Hayden Taylor
Quest for Fire, by Lenore Keeshig-Tobias
First Love, by Diane Debassige
Lupi, The Great White Wolf, by Esther Jacko
Someday, by Drew Hayden Taylor
20ᵗʰ Century Indian Boy, by Mark Seabrook
New Voices Woman, by Larry E. Lewis
If Jesus Met Nanabush, by Alanis King
The Manitoulin Incident, by Alanis King
The Tommy Prince Story, by Alanis King
The Best Medicine Show, Collective Creation
The Lost Warrior, by Darrel Manitowabi
Broken Snowshoe Moon, by Amie-Lyn Ominika
Biidaasigekwe, Sunlight Woman, texts by Angeline Williams
The Peace Tree, Collective Creation

SKY, An Aboriginal Dance Drama, Collective Creation
Please Do Not Touch the Indians, by Joseph A. Dandurand
The Jerry Jessie Jones Show, Collective Creation
Toronto@Dreamer'sRock.com, by Drew Hayden Taylor
New World Brave, Collective Creation
The Dreaming Beauty, based on the short story by Daniel David Moses
Ever! That Nanabush!, based on "Legends of Nanabush" as retold
    and illustrated by Daphne Odjig
A Trickster Tale, by Tomson Highway
Myths That Unite Us, collaboration between De-ba-jeh-mu-jig,
    Studio Ypsilon (Prague, Czech Republic), and the Drama Program
    at the University of Toronto at Scarborough
Billy, by Chris Craddock
Hamlet, with Toronto's Soulpepper Theatre, presented by
    De-ba-jeh-mu-jig
Your Dream Was Mine, by Shirley Cheechoo and Greta Cheechoo
The Gift, by Joe Osawabine, Elisha Sidlar, and Paula Wing
The Promise (dance piece), directed and choreographed by Karen
    Pheasant
The Indian Affairs, Group Creation
How Will You Remember Me?, by Joe Osawbine and Elisha Sidlar
Shtaa-taa-haa! Nanabush!, French adaptation by Geneviève Pineault of
    Ever! That Nanabush
Biidaasigekwe, Sunlight Woman (in English and Ojibway), texts by
    Angeline Williams
The Meeting (dance and movement), by Bruce Naokwegijig (stilt
    walking) and Spirit Synott (wheelchair dance)
The Art of Living, collaboration between De-ba-jeh-mu-jig, Studio
    Ypsilon (Prague), and the Drama Program at the University of
    Toronto at Scarborough
The Seven Grandfather Teachings, Commissioned Collective Creation,
    led by Joe Osawabine
The Four Axes (movement piece), Collective Creation led and
    choreographed by Bruce Naokwegijig

Four Directions Creation Process

4D is a unique process for creating new works developed by De-ba-jeh-mu-jig Theatre Group over a span of four years (1996–2000). Holistic in nature, 4D is a culturally and socially specific process that identifies the artist as the creation, and performance as the celebration. 4D recognizes that as humans we create with our entire being—physical, emotional, intellectual, and our spiritual selves, and therefore it accepts and specifically supports the artist in all four of these areas. 4D is adapted to the skills and intuitions of artists who have been strongly influenced by an oral tradition, it is a process that nurtures honesty more than accuracy, and sharing more than starring, and it is a process that consciously uses personal resources, physical—like a skill, emotional—like a memory, spiritual—like an experience, and intellectual—like an object, as the key to personal and group creation.

Works Cited

Behrisch, Erika. "On the Trail of an Arctic Tale: Tracing Sir John Franklin in Charles Dickens and Wilkie Collins's *The Frozen Deep*." *Storytelling: Interdisciplinary and Intercultural Perspectives*. Ed. Irene Maria F. Blayer and Monica Sanchez. New York: Peter Lang, 2002. 58–71.

Blaeser, Kimberly M. "Writing voices speaking: Native authors and an oral aesthetic." *Talking on the Page: Editing Aboriginal Oral Texts*. Ed. Laura J. Murray and Keren Rice. Toronto: U of Toronto P, 1999. 53–68.

Blayer, Irene Maria F., and Monica Sanchez. Preface. *Storytelling*. xi.

Cameron, Margaret M. "Play-acting in Canada during the French Regime." *Canadian Historical Review* XI.1 (March 1930): 9–19.

Campbell, Maria. Interview. *Contemporary Challenges: Conversations with Canadian Native Authors*. Ed. Hartmut Lutz. Saskatoon: Fifth House, 1991. 41–65.

Cruikshank, Julie. *The Social Life of Stories: Narrative and Knowledge in the Yukon Territory*. Lincoln: U of Nebraska P, 1998.

Cuthand, Beth. Interview. *Contemporary Challenges: Conversations with Canadian Native Authors*. 33–40.

Erskine, Michael. "De-baj blends traditions old and new." *Manitoulin Island: The Natural Destination*. Winter/spring 2003. 3.

———. "New creative space a boost for oldest town." *Manitoulin Island*. 6.

Filewod, Alan. *Performing Canada: The Nation Enacted in the Imagined Theatre*. Textual Studies in Canada 15. Spring 2002. Monograph Series: Critical Performance/s in Canada. Ed. James Hoffman and Katherine Sutherland. U College of the Cariboo, B.C.

Greenslade, Frances. *A Pilgrim in Ireland: A Quest for Home*. Toronto: Penguin, 2002.

Highway, Tomson. *The Rez Sisters*. Saskatoon: Fifth House, 1988.

———. "Who is the Trickster?" Playbill for *A Trickster Tale*. De-ba-jeh-mu-jig Theatre Group. Summer 2003. 2–3.

Johnston, Denis W. "Lines and Circles: The 'Rez' Plays of Tomson Highway." *Canadian Literature* 124–25 (Spring/Summer 1990): 254–64.

Manossa, Geraldine. "The Beginning of Cree Performance Culture." *(Ad)dressing Our Words: Aboriginal Perspectives on Aboriginal Literatures.* Ed. Armand Garnet Ruffo. Penticton, B.C.: Theytus Books, 2001. 169–80.

McLeod, Neal. "Coming Home Through Stories." *(Ad)dressing Our Words.* 17–36.

Preston, Jennifer. "Weesageechak Begins to Dance: Native Earth Performing Arts Inc." *The Drama Review* 36.1 (T133). Spring 1992: 135–59.

Stone, Kay. "Stones on the Mountain: Crossing Borders into a Story." *Storytelling.* 1–13.

Sturm, Brian W. "Lost in a Story: Modeling Storytelling and Storylistening." *Storytelling.* 14–26.

Index

photo by Karl Skierszkan

Shannon Hengen is a Professor of English at Laurentian University. Her teaching roles include modern and contemporary drama, American literature, women's writing, and the writer's voice. She is also involved in the Interdisciplinary Masters in Humanities. Current research interests are Aboriginal and testimonial theatre, and Margaret Atwood's oeuvre.

She thanks the editors and publisher of Playwrights Canada Press and editor Dr. Lisa Laframboise of Sudbury for the care taken with this book.